CONTENTS

D0291397

EMPLOYED for
LIFE

DEVOTIONAL

BARBARA
RARDEN

DEDICATION

To my amazing and wonderful children—Steve, Amy and Katy.

Steve—I am so proud of the man you have become
and your service to others.

Amy—You bring me joy! Thanks for all the time and talent
you've invested in my many projects.

Katy—What a gift you are in my life!

May you and your families always walk in the
truth of God's love and in His manifest blessing.

Employed for Life Devotional

Copyright © 2012 by Barbara Rarden. All rights reserved.

No part of this publication may be reproduced, stored in a retrieval system or transmitted in any way by any means, electronic, mechanical, photocopy, recording, or otherwise without the prior permission of the author except as provided by USA copyright law.

ISBN: 978-1-56427-304-8

Category: Religious / Christian Living / Devotional

Published in cooperation with Crown Financial Ministries, Inc.

Cover and Layout Designs: Sean Allen

Unless otherwise indicated, all Scripture quotations a e taken from The Holy Bible, New International Version®. Copyright © 1973, 1978, 19. 4 by Biblica. Used by permission of Zondervan Publishing House. All rights reserved.

Scripture quotations marked "NLT" are taken from The Holy Bible, New Living Translation. Copyright © 1996, 2004, 2007 by Tyndale House Foundation. Used by permission of Tyndale House Publishers, Inc. Carol Stream, Illinois 60188. All rights reserved.

Scripture quotations marked "NKJV" are taken from The Holy Bible, New King James Version. Copyright © 1982 by Thomas Nelson, Inc. Used by permission. All rights reserved.

Printed in the United States of America.

April 2012 edition

PREFACE

Have you seen Jesus lately? Have you seen Him in the workplace? Whether you knew it or not He was with you when you received that lay-off notice, ready to sustain and comfort you. He was there too when you went out of your way to be of service and no one noticed. Jesus is always standing beside you as you experience those awful jitters before a big presentation, with whispers of encouragement. He's there when you're passed over for a promotion and when you're the one promoted. The world may talk about the importance of separating Church and State, keeping the spiritual and natural apart, but that's simply impossible in the lives of believers because the Holy Spirit of God actually lives within every believer. The Spirit of God goes with us into every work environment and is available to help in every situation. Jesus is with you; He always has been and He always will be. But do you know it? Have you seen Him lately? Do you recognize His responses to your prayers or have you passed them off as coincidences like so many others do?

These aren't silly or casual questions. In His day, many saw Jesus face to face and didn't recognize who He was. His disciples didn't recognize Him on the Emmaus road or on the Galilee shore. Today there are many who know about Jesus, who met Him at their salvation, but who have never fully entered into the rich, deep, and personal relationship that Jesus seeks with them. They attend church and do many of the "right things" without the joy and benefit of experiencing His presence and personality. If He's entered their hearts at all, they've kept Him on the front porch, so to speak. Things are too crazy, situations too challenging, and evil too strong for followers of Jesus to try to go it alone with an occasional glance in the Lord's direction. If you're a believer who doesn't really *know* Jesus, you're in trouble. Not just spiritually but in this natural realm too—especially in the workplace.

This devotional was written to help you, His employee, develop an intimate, personal relationship with Jesus. On two momentous occasions God broke dramatically into this earthly realm to tell us to *listen to His Son, Jesus* (Matthew 17:5, Mark 9:6-8). He is the way, the truth and the life. In

Him you will find answers to all your questions about life, and that includes work. But to have the relationship that God intends, it isn't sufficient to place Jesus in the center of your life and plans. You must instead fit your entire life into Him. Your victory in this life depends upon entering into His will and abiding there. So for the next 90 days—the standard probationary period in the workplace—you'll have an opportunity to listen, attend to, and apply the words of Jesus in your life and work. And it really doesn't matter if you're in the workplace or temporarily out of it because, as a believer, you are employed by God for life!

Not only do you need that close relationship with Jesus, the world needs your strong connection with Him too. Workers struggling in the darkness need a demonstration of the power and authority of the name of Jesus, the Light of the World. Get ready to meet Jesus every day, to grow in your relationship with Him, and to receive your work assignments directly from the heart of God. Nothing matters more in this orientation process than you gaining a deeper knowledge of Jesus as your Lord, Master and Friend and a clearer awareness of your place in His workplace.

May the fullness of God's blessing be upon you as you join Jesus to reach the workplace with the Good News of the Kingdom of God, one position at a time!

A word about format...

At the start of each week you'll find a high level overview of your focus and objectives for the upcoming week. Each day you'll read a scripture by Jesus and a brief devotional on the day's topic. I hope you'll spend some time thinking about and meditating on what you've read. "Meditation is the activity of calling to mind, and thinking over, and dwelling on, and applying to oneself, the various things that one knows about the works and ways and purposes and promises of God. It is an activity of holy thought, consciously performed in the presence of God, by the help of God, as a means of communication with God. Its purpose is to clear one's mental and spiritual vision of God, and to let His truth make its full and proper impact on one's mind and heart." [1]

Then in keeping with Jesus' instructions, **Speak it out** statements have been provided to give you the opportunity to appropriate, as your own, the truths presented in the daily reading. *"What I tell you in the dark, speak in the daylight; what is whispered in your ear, proclaim from the roofs"* (Matthew 10:27).

The apostle Paul tells us in Romans 10:17, *"Consequently, faith comes from hearing the message, and the message is heard through the word of Christ."* As you read aloud and agree with what you've just heard from the Lord, you *"build yourself up in your most holy faith"* (Jude 1:20).

In the **Walk it out** sections you'll find practical applications that will enable you to put the instructions for the day into immediate practice in your workplace or employment search process.

---

[1] J.I. Packer, *Knowing God*, InterVarsity Press, Downers Grove, IL, 1973, p. 23.

INTRODUCTION

> *"A voice came from the cloud, saying,*
> *'This is my Son, whom I have chosen;*
> *listen to him.'"*
>
> - LUKE 9:35

Imagine that you have just been hired. Soon you'll be starting your first day of work so you're beginning to feel those new employee jitters. You're probably wondering how you'll ever learn all you need to know in order to perform the work you're assigned. Who knows how long it will take before you no longer feel like the "new kid"? If you can recall the last time you started a new work assignment I'm sure you can identify with what I'm describing and all the thoughts that flooded your mind at the start of your new job.

As you pick up this devotional, though, you may not be feeling these jitters. You may believe yourself to be currently unemployed and still looking for your next assignment. Or perhaps you already have a job and today seems just like more of the same old thing at work. But guess what? Right now—if you choose—you can start working for God in His Kingdom, with assignments, opportunities and benefits you can't even imagine. Of course, you'll also face great challenges in joining this company. In fact, if it were not for the resources, support and training provided by this Employer, you would stand no chance of success at all—at least not by His standards. But don't worry, He's got you covered!

This Employer, your Heavenly Father, has wanted you to work in His family business since the day you were born. You cannot imagine His joy at knowing you just might show up one day for full-time work. In preparation, He has put the word out that you are to be given anything and everything required to make you successful. You are to be trained carefully and thoroughly so that you will be able to assume a significant, future leadership position that already has your name on it! But don't misunderstand—you won't be coddled or babied in any way. The training and preparation you will experience will be intense, like a military boot camp. It is training God considers so important that He has assigned His Son, Jesus Himself, as your direct supervisor. You couldn't be in better hands!

This is your Orientation to Kingdom employment and it is not a trial run or probationary period. You have been recruited and hired into a position of absolute job security. Unlike the employment options of the world, retirement, lay off, business failure, and termination are not options. This Employer has actually adopted you into His family, not just hired you into the family business! You will never be disowned either; God has chosen you to be His forever.

What's your part in this employment arrangement? Well, you can apply yourself with all the energy and passion you've got, or you can drag your feet; you can fight for control over your career, or you can quickly relinquish control and discover the wonderful surprises God has in store for you. The faster you plunge all the way into His work environment, the faster you'll discover how awesome it is to serve in the employ of the King of Kings. For His part, your Employer and Father, God Almighty, promises: *"He who began a good work in you will carry it on to completion until the day of Christ Jesus"* (Philippians 1:6).

Welcome aboard! The first day of your Kingdom assignment begins now.

WEEK 1

BATTLE FOR THE WORKPLACE

"And from the days of John the Baptist until now the kingdom of heaven suffers violence, and the violent take it by force."

- MATTHEW 11:12

There's a spiritual battle being fought over the workplace. The true followers of Christ are warring against the forces of the Enemy and the kingdoms of this world. At stake are the hearts of workers including, unfortunately, the hearts of many believers who don't even realize they've been taken captive in this battle. That statement may strike you as odd; you may be wondering how hearts could be won or lost in the workplace when most of the time hearts seem to be nowhere in sight.

But the truth is that the workplace has become an idol in the lives of countless workers. They spend all their time, energy and talents trying to build empires, create reputations, amass fortunes, and gain status by serving the gods of the workplace for the treasures they think they'll find there. Seduced by attractions in the world's kingdoms and deceived by the Enemy, they now live to work or work to live. In their hearts there is little or no room for their Creator and Provider to participate in their employment experience.

It doesn't have to be that way. God desires to be fully engaged in your employment experience. He wants to join forces with you, whatever your current circumstance—unemployment, misemployment or successful employment. He even has a job description just for you that will allow you to enjoy all the benefits of Kingdom life as you fulfill your destiny in Christ. If you accept His offer He'll provide everything you need to triumph in the workplace, lead in eternity and experience wholeness and true abundant life. This is His intention for all who come to work full time in His "family business." What you do with that awesome offer will be up to you.

By the way, God is the only One who is willing and able to pull us out of this workplace mess and rescue us from the Enemy's deception and world's economy. He sent Jesus to accomplish that purpose 2,000 years ago and is still in the redemption business today! Believers have only to follow Jesus as He makes a way for each of us. Here's His first, start-up instruction. *"Love the Lord your God with all your heart and with all your soul and with all your mind"* (Matthew 22:37). For you see, there simply is no place for divided loyalty on the battlefield. That gives you an idea of the gravity of the topics we'll be looking at this week. If you're ready to begin…

SPEAK IT OUT:

· I fight on the side of the Kingdom of God. I choose to follow Jesus into this spiritual battle.

· By faith I turn my mind, will and emotions toward God and give Him all my love and loyalty.

· My heart is fixed on eternity, and I will not be deceived by the things of this world.

My Journal Notes

 DAY TWO KINGDOMS, ONE TRUE KING

*"No servant can serve two masters; for either he
will hate the one and love the other, or else he will be
loyal to the one and despise the other. You cannot serve
God and mammon."*

- LUKE 16:13 NKJV

We live our lives in the presence of these two entirely different kingdoms today. The Kingdom of God has its foundation in the eternal spiritual realm. If you are unclear about the term "Kingdom of God" it simply refers to a life or condition completely submitted to the rule of God and His will. Mammon, the world's kingdom, is based here in the temporary, earthly realm. And, while God's Kingdom is an invisible kingdom, make no mistake—it is more real and permanent than the kingdom of this world. For this reason Jesus calls us to put our trust in God's spiritual Kingdom to meet both our natural and our spiritual needs. The world's kingdom and its "riches" cannot be trusted to satisfy either!

Countless job seekers have accepted Jesus as their Lord and Savior without understanding how God's truth can impact their work life. They don't know how to integrate the spiritual power of God into life's practical circumstances, so they end up trying to walk by faith while holding onto the beliefs and behaviors of the world. If you are in that group, this devotional is for you. Spend these 90 days listening to Jesus as He explains what God sent Him to accomplish, what happened because of His death and Resurrection and how you can become like Him as you go through your day-to-day life.

What you will discover, if you don't already know it, is that: "(Religion) must occupy the whole of life. There is no question of a compromise between the claims of God and the claims of culture, or politics, or anything else. God's claim is infinite and inexorable. You can refuse it: or you can begin to try to grant it. There is no middle way. Yet in spite of this Christianity does not exclude any of the ordinary human activities. St Paul tells people to get on with their jobs."[2] If you are ready to get on with it and learn how to experience victory, peace and joy in your life and work...

SPEAK IT OUT:

· By faith I trust my life to Jesus Christ and claim my citizenship in the Kingdom of God.

· My loyalty is not divided. I serve God and Him only.

· My focus is on eternity and my goal is to glorify God with my life and work.

WALK IT OUT:

Checkbook Audit: Would you like to see which Kingdom has your allegiance, or had it when you were last in the workplace? Today money represents treasure and the words of Jesus still apply: *"For where your treasure is, there your heart will be also."* So take out your checkbook register for any three-month period of employment and look at where you spent your money. Now don't misunderstand, the issue is not what possessions you have but rather what possessions have you! How many hours did you work each week simply in order to secure and support your possessions?

This activity illustrates how work and workplace activities can invade the lives of believers and crowd out the things of God. The great news is

---

[2] C.S. Lewis, *The Weight of Glory and Other Addresses*, Macmillan, New York, NY, 1980, p. 25.

that a season away from the workplace, or a difficult employment situation, can provide the perfect opportunity to rededicate yourself to God and His Kingdom and get your career on the right track.

My Journal Notes

DAY 2   IT'S ABOUT THE HEART

"You are the ones who justify yourselves in the eyes of others, but God knows your hearts. What is highly valued among men is detestable in God's sight."

- LUKE 16:15

Work itself is not our problem. There is no dispute that God created man to be fruitful and responsible for the cultivation of the earth through productive effort. *"I know that there is nothing better for men than to be happy and to do good while they live. That everyone may eat and drink, and find satisfaction in all his toil—this is the gift of God"* (Ecclesiastes 3:12-13).

Man was designed for work and, in working, to find satisfaction. But we now live in a fallen world that has corrupted God's original purpose for work. Over time men were led to believe that work itself was the source of happiness, satisfaction, sustenance and purpose; obtaining things became the purpose for expending effort and talent, not doing good or being fruitful. A subtle and persistent distraction diverted attention from mankind's true Source and Provider to the world's glittering counterfeits—money, leisure, indulgence, comfort and pleasure. Jesus acknowledged the effectiveness of this snare with the words: *"I tell you the truth, it is hard for a rich man to enter the kingdom of heaven"* (Matthew 19:23).

"It is not what a man does that determines whether his work is sacred or secular, it is why he does it. The motive is everything." [3] Money isn't the problem either—it's certainly no sin to acquire wealth. Rather, it's the love of money that's deadly! Again, it's all about the heart. "We must learn to

---

[3] A.W. Tozer, *The Pursuit of God*, Christian Publications, Camp Hill, PA, p. 127.

measure ourselves, not by our knowledge about God, not by our gifts and responsibilities in the church, but by how we pray and what goes on in our hearts. Many of us, I suspect, have no idea how impoverished we are at this level. Let us ask the Lord to show us."[4]

When you examine your work objectives, make sure God's will is at the heart of all you do and think. If it's not, and you want to change that now...

 SPEAK IT OUT:

- I willingly let go of anything that prevents me from walking closely with Christ.

- I am no longer interested in the ways of this world, for I know they are only a distraction.

- I surrender my life—body, soul and spirit— to Jesus Christ.

 WALK IT OUT:

Objective Statements: What are you looking for? How do you describe the position you aspire to? There are the words you'll say out loud when asked this question, and then there are words you'll have only in your mind, perhaps spoken only to God. Pay attention to your response to this question. Consider your motives and what your objective statement reveals about your heart. Are you asking potential employers to meet your needs, or are you offering to meet theirs? Write your Objective Statement from the employer's point of view.

Are you asking God to provide a certain salary, choice assignment, or prestigious title? If so, the world's economy may still be exerting its influence on your thoughts. God promises to provide what is required to accomplish

---

[4] J.I. Packer, *Knowing God,* InterVarsity Press, Downer's Grover, IL, 1973, p. 32.

the destiny He has assigned you, not to satisfy a self-focused wish list. Rethink your employment objectives to bring God glory, demonstrate your stewardship of the resources He's given you and meet the needs of your family—an assignment that will enable you to serve others and be a blessing. That'll be a good start.

My Journal Notes

My Journal Notes

DAY **YOU'VE BEEN CHOSEN**

"You did not choose Me, but I chose you and
appointed you that you should go and bear fruit,
fruit that will last....
As it is, you do not belong to the world, but
I have chosen you out of the world.
That is why the world hates you."

- JOHN 15:16, 19

By God's grace we have been drawn to His Son and have accepted Him as our Savior. In so doing we agreed to make Him Lord and Master over everything, including our work lives. Now Jesus expects you to follow His direction, perform the work He assigns and act in obedience to His will. This isn't just a good idea—it's absolutely essential. The moment you crossed over into the Kingdom of God, the world "kicked you out." Perhaps you, like many other believers, noticed how your work became more difficult after you were saved, how old methods no longer worked like they used to. In fact, your "luck" (a device of the world) did indeed run out.

The apostle Paul describes the group from which, by God's grace, you've been separated: *"For men will be lovers of themselves, lovers of money, boasters, proud, blasphemers, disobedient to parents, unthankful, unholy, unloving, unforgiving, slanderers, without self-control, brutal, despisers of good, traitors, headstrong, haughty, lovers of pleasure rather than lovers of God, having a form of godliness but denying its power. And from such people turn away"* (2 Timothy 3:2-5 NKJV). It's clear you cannot stay in that world kingdom and prosper spiritually.

God is ready to provide a type of prosperity and wholeness that the world with all its luck could never deliver. You will bear fruit and walk in the strength of the Lord and the power of His might by quickly responding in obedience to His commands. So, while it is possible to remain out on the "fringe" of the Kingdom, never realizing the benefits of serving the Kingdom to the fullest measure possible, it's really dangerous. Remember you're not in neutral territory—there's a battle going on. *"Your enemy the devil prowls around like a roaring lion looking for someone to devour"* (1 Peter 5:8). Instead of simply "hoping for the best," accept your election into God's Kingdom and His workplace, commit to learning this new way of life, and…

Speak it out:

· I praise God that I have been chosen and adopted into His family!

· By faith I accept God's assignment and purpose for my life.

· My focus is on eternity and my goal is to glorify God with my life and work.

Walk it out:

Posture and Presentation: Before you go anywhere today, take the time to stand in front of a full-length mirror, if possible. Check your posture. Do you stand tall and straight like a person of royalty? Do you walk with a confident gait and uplifted eyes? Would people watching as you walk by think that you must have something special going on to look so happy and at peace? It's up to you to adopt behaviors befitting a child chosen and adopted by the Most High God. Start practicing now to look like a representative of the Kingdom of God wherever you go.

My Journal Notes

DAY 4   COUNT THE COST

"And whoever does not bear his cross and
come after Me cannot be My disciple.
For which of you, intending to build a tower,
does not sit down first and count the cost,
whether he has enough to finish it? …
So likewise, whoever of you does not forsake
all that he has cannot be My disciple."

- LUKE 14:27-33 NKJV

Do you recall the story of the rich young ruler who walked away from Jesus after being told to sell all his possessions? Clearly, he counted the cost of discipleship and found it too great a price to pay. On the other hand, Jesus also tells the stories of those who considered the Kingdom, represented as treasure and a pearl, to be of such value that they joyfully sold everything to obtain it. The common denominator in these stories is that the Kingdom of God requires the surrender of everything. You accepted Jesus as your Savior and your Lord; you agreed to give Him your life in response to His salvation.

It's unlikely that you'll be asked to relinquish all your possessions, but if they are preventing you from receiving God's best, prepare to be challenged as was the rich young ruler. Since your Creator knows what He designed you to do, He also might ask you to change your career direction or the way you work. As your Lord and Master, Jesus has every right to ask for anything He chooses and expect your obedience. He paid for you with His life.

The amazing thing is this: While your life as a disciple of Jesus Christ will cause you to give up your own tiny plans and small thinking, it will open you to a life you would not have imagined before in your biggest dreams. You only have to give up your attachment to the world's counterfeit riches to receive a life that is real, abundant and eternal. As C.S. Lewis put it, "Now is our chance to choose the right side. God is holding back to give us that chance. It won't last forever. We must take it or leave it."[5] Start now, and…

SPEAK IT OUT:

· In faith I build my life on the rock of Jesus Christ.

· Jesus is my Lord, Savior and Master, and I surrender all that I have to Him.

· I believe that God is good and that He loves me perfectly. I trust Him with my life.

WALK IT OUT:

Investment Strategy: Very few things of real value can be obtained without paying a high price for them. If the job of your dreams requires training or education you don't have, get it! If you need to speak another language or get some additional experience to equip yourself for your next opportunity, do it. Don't focus on how hard it will be to achieve—if it's really important and God is in it, it will be worth the effort. The same is true of spiritual development, faith grows over time as it is applied and tested. Begin your spiritual investment strategy now. Practice self-control, offer forgiveness and develop kindness. Over time you'll see the value of paying the price day-by-day.

---

[5] C.S. Lewis, Mere Christianity, Macmillan Publishing Co., New York, NY, 1960 p. 66.

My Journal Notes

WHO ARE YOU TODAY?

"You are my friends if you do what I command.
I no longer call you servants, because
a servant does not know his master's business.
Instead, I have called you friends,
for everything that I learned from my
Father I have made known to you."

- JOHN 15:14-15

Think about the story called The Prodigal Son. The younger son demanded that his father turn over his portion of the family inheritance early. Then, because he lacked the character to handle it, he ended up in a pigpen. Meantime, his older brother worked day after day expecting to be acknowledged and rewarded for his self-righteous efforts. He appears never to have tapped the available resources to bless others or to enjoy time with his father. Both sons had their eyes solely on themselves and their self-centeredness brought them misery. Even today many believers are so sure they know what's best for themselves that they pray only to get God to deliver on their demands. Are you in this group?

If you're still trying to figure out your own path and career goals, you need to change your mind about your approach to employment. You simply cannot achieve meaning and satisfaction in this life until you get your eyes off yourself and your situation. Jesus will reveal the Father's heart and right priorities for your life and work. If you'll follow Him, He'll share everything He knows about the "family business," lead you to accomplish your personal destiny and—imagine this—become your close personal friend!

"The sovereign God wants to be loved for Himself and honored for Himself, but that is only part of what He wants. The other part is that He wants us to know that when we have Him we have everything – we have all the rest."[6] If you're ready to stop living a self-centered life and enter into the greatest friendship you'll ever experience…

Speak it out:

· I trust God's timing in my life. He knows what I need and when I need it.

· By faith I participate in God's turnaround strategies whenever I need them in my life.

· God is working everything together for my good because I love Him and I'm following where He leads.

Walk it out:

Turnaround Strategies: God has strategies that He works in the lives of His children. Take a few moments to reflect on your current employment situation and ask Jesus to reveal the Father's heart:

1. Has a recent job change removed you from an abusive, exhausting or dangerous work situation? Are you in need of a rescue?

2. Is there a relationship or need in your life that needs your priority attention and time?

3. Is there a new type of work you've felt led to pursue but haven't done anything about it yet?

4. Is there a significant project or ministry that needs your talent and time in a volunteer effort?

---

[6] A.W. Tozer, *The Attributes of God*, Vol. 1, Wingspread Publications, Camp Hill, PA, p. 120.

These are just some of the signals that an employment change may be needed. Is there a change you need to make? Can you recognize God working in your life right now? He definitely desires abundant life for you. Ask how you can cooperate with His plans for you.

My Journal Notes

WEEK

KINGDOM LANGUAGE

*"You are permitted to understand the secrets of the
Kingdom of Heaven, but others are not.
To those who listen to my teaching, more
understanding will be given, and they will have
an abundance of knowledge.
But for those who are not listening,
even what little understanding they have
will be taken away from them."*

— MATTHEW 13:11-12 NLT

*"Jesus spoke all these things to the crowd in parables; he
did not say anything to them without using a parable.
So was fulfilled what was spoken through the prophet:
'I will open my mouth in parables, I will utter things
hidden since the creation of the world.'"*

— MATTHEW 13:34

Think of it like this, you've moved to a new country and the language spoken there is different from your native tongue. To become effective in this new place you must master its language. Now, realize that Jesus is the Word of God. He is the language of the Kingdom of God. The Bible is God's Word and Jesus is the living Word whose voice you can learn to hear behind the words you read in the Bible. According to Jesus the Holy Spirit, given to you at salvation, is your connection to His Word and Wisdom (John 14:26). So, if you desire to be successful in the Kingdom workplace, dive into the Word until you can speak the language of the Kingdom fluently.

You will learn things from Jesus that have been hidden from the rest of mankind. Clearly His ways are not our ways, so we won't just accidentally discover them. But by His grace, believers have been offered understanding of the secrets of the Kingdom of Heaven! Notice the wording, however: "permitted to understand" and "given understanding." The door has been unlocked. Now it's up to you to make the investment in reading the Word, asking the Holy Spirit's assistance as you do, so that you will be able to access the understanding you'll need to live as God intended. If you desire to keep the understanding you now have and grow into the abundance of knowledge Jesus offers, your commitment to listening and learning is imperative.

To get you started, this week you'll study the "master parable" of the sower (Mark 4). It provides a foundation for understanding how the Kingdom of God operates. As you study it, you'll also be reminded of the forces that work against it. Get ready to discover how ignorance of the Word can cause you to miss critically important instructions from God and how neglecting it will cause you to crumble when the pressure's on. Take God's Word deep into your heart and mind; guard it and keep it from being overrun and overridden by worldly distractions. Finally, you'll be shown the process that will enable you to receive everything God wants you to know, to derive the benefit of the hidden wisdom and guidance He's prepared to share. With care your heart can become the fertile soil required for a fruitful and productive life.

It takes hard, continuous work to produce a harvest. In Jesus, the Word of God in human form, God has provided the "incorruptible seed" that never fails. What do you plan to do with it? If you'd like to reap what God has in mind for you...

SPEAK IT OUT:

· By faith I receive understanding of the Word whenever I read it.

· I expect to receive wisdom from God that the world does not know.

· I am God's child, a citizen of the Kingdom, and God's ways are not a mystery to me.

My Journal Notes

My Journal Notes

DAY 1   STOLEN SEEDS

"Listen then to what the parable of the sower
means: When anyone hears the message about
the kingdom and does not understand it,
the evil one comes and snatches away
what was sown in his heart.
This is the seed sown along the path."

- MATTHEW 13:18-19

Jesus told the disciples that He intentionally spoke in parables so that His followers would understand what He was telling them and those who rejected Him would not. He intended to offer His followers divine wisdom that would enable them to experience the blessings of God's Kingdom in this life and the next. But, as you can see in today's verse, if you don't understand what He's saying when you hear it, a very real Enemy will steal God's messages right out of your heart and you'll never know what you've lost.

You can't forget that you are in the middle of a battle. Your Enemy does not want you to receive battle plans or learn the tactics that will enable you to rise above the world systems he has so carefully constructed. You'll have to be vigilant to look and listen for God's voice in everything that goes on around you. It's up to you to work, and work hard, to gain an understanding of the Kingdom through the life of Jesus. *"Get wisdom. Though it cost all you have, get understanding"* (Proverbs 4:7).

Today, many believers are content to pay only casual attention to God's voice through His Word, and as a result they fail to recognize His answers to their prayers and daily walk away from opportunities for abundant life. Clearly, you can't depend on God's promises if you don't even know what they are. If you don't learn what Jesus has to say about life, work and purpose, you'll easily become ensnared and lost in the world's system and workplace. To avoid this...

SPEAK IT OUT:

- I give God my full attention and expect to hear His calling. I am determined to hang on to His Word.

- By faith I receive His promises to provide all I need as I seek after His Kingdom and righteousness.

- I believe that God's will for me is far better than anything the world has to offer.

WALK IT OUT:

Decision Power: Make a habit of noticing every decision you make throughout the day. Pause and ask God for His insight and direction on every choice from the smallest to the biggest. That's right, every decision! Practice listening for a response from the Holy Spirit within you. Take the time to search God's Word to see what guidance you can find that applies to your situation. Time spent in the New Testament is especially important in order to gain a full understanding of the *"better covenant established on better promises"* that has been given to believers through Jesus Christ (Hebrews 8:6 NKJV). This is the process that will renew your mind and transform your life (Romans 12:2). When you do things by rote or take actions without thinking, you run the risk of behaving like the world. Don't let your learned behaviors rob you of the power of making godly decisions. Wrong decisions lead to actions and habits that will carry you far away from God's perfect plan for your life.

My Journal Notes

DAY 2   GOOD FOR THE MOMENT

"The one who received the seed that fell on rocky places is the man who hears the word and at once receives it with joy. But since he has no root, he lasts only a short time. When trouble or persecution comes because of the word, he quickly falls away."

- MATTHEW 13:20-21

Who can't relate to this scripture? You've probably experienced some wonderful times when you felt the presence of the Lord and the joy that accompanies it. There are life experiences that bring us close to God—the birth of a healthy, beautiful baby, a stunning sunset, the sudden appearance of a glorious rainbow after a storm. Then life crashes in and God seems to move far, far away. Are you feeling the effects of "rocky ground living" now? Do you believe that you cannot make it another week if you don't get a job or that you cannot endure one more day in your current position? You probably don't want to hear this, but the only way faith grows deeper roots is if it is stretched and tested—sometimes to the very end of supplies, money and hope.

To get back on track, take God's Word, find New Testament promises that address your situation, and begin to meditate on them. Listen for God's voice to speak through His Word. You probably won't hear an audible voice from Heaven but you may find a scripture that speaks to your situation or hear a sermon that provides the wisdom you need. Through some means God will quicken your understanding and show you how to deal with your circumstances and questions. Spend time reviewing all the examples of Jesus intervening in natural circumstances to meet the needs of those who sought

Him. In this way you will nurture the "incorruptible seed" that's been planted in your heart and help its roots to go deeper. Be assured, by the very words of the Living Word, Jesus, that as long as you are listening and obeying to the best of your ability, you will see His hand in your circumstances. Soon the rocky ground described in the parable will no longer apply to you. In commitment to nurturing God's Word in your heart…

SPEAK IT OUT:

· I receive the Word of God with joy and hold on to it.

· I am not moved by what I see or hear in this world. My focus remains on His promises.

· By faith I trust in Jesus to get me through every storm of life.

WALK IT OUT:

Settle Down: What's your personal process for settling down so that you can hear from God and experience His peace? Don't have one? Well, make that today's assignment. Perhaps you can settle your mind by taking a long walk or a bike ride. Do whatever you need to do to find a way to become really quiet. To take control of your thoughts, try writing each idea, worry or stray thought down as soon as it crosses your mind. Tell yourself you'll get to it later and return your focus to the Lord. Do this consistently and, over time, you will be able to settle down in the toughest of circumstances.

My Journal Notes

DAY 3 CHOKED BY CARES

> *"The one who received the seed that fell among the thorns is the man who hears the word, but the worries of this life ... choke it, making it unfruitful."*
>
> - MATTHEW 13:22

Worrying is a choice—a decision to doubt God's Word—and doing so makes the Word unfruitful. It is one thing to be ignorant of the Word of God, but in this case Jesus is referring to someone who actually hears it, understands what's being said, and then allows life's worries to choke it out and render it useless. Of course, this is bad news for the believers who do this because they forfeit what the Word would have produced in their lives.

This conscious choice is also disrespectful of God. How can any believer justify such an affront—to discount the power and authority of God's Word and allow His precious promises to be overruled and overpowered by the lies of the world? Perhaps the apostle John answers the question in 1 John 4:18 when he states: *"There is no fear in love; but perfect love casts out fear... But he who fears has not been made perfect in love."* You must have the direct and personal experience of God's extraordinary love to conquer worry and anxiety. If you haven't experienced God's love in this way, ask Jesus to become real for you.

If you have experienced God's love in a real and personal way, ask yourself what on earth would God have to do that He has not already done for you to anchor your confidence in His ability to deal with every problem that you will ever face? Think about it, how can you possibly trust God enough to spend all eternity with Him and yet not trust Him enough to stop worrying about your employment circumstances and daily needs? If you know that God is worthy of your complete confidence and trust...

SPEAK IT OUT:

· I am guarded by Almighty God. He never takes His eyes off me.

· By faith I believe that I will be victorious in life because Christ always leads me in triumph. *(2 Corinthians 2:14)*

· I act in obedience to the Lord's instruction and with boldness, knowing the Holy Spirit is backing me up.

WALK IT OUT:

Why Worry? Take time today to reflect on the actual act of worrying. Can you identify any time when you came up with a solution by worrying about a problem? What processes have you used successfully to solve a problem? Was worrying any part of that process? If you're completely honest you'll probably conclude that worrying has never produced value in your life. Does it make sense to keep doing something when it is clearly unproductive? God's instruction is clear: don't fret or worry—ever. But the choice is yours. You can decide to banish worry from your thinking and to ask the Holy Spirit to help you do it. You'll be amazed at how much this will free your mind for creative thinking.

My Journal Notes

DAY 4 RUINED BY RICHES

"The one who received the seed that fell among the thorns is the man who hears the word, but the … deceitfulness of wealth choke[s] it, making it unfruitful."

- MATTHEW 13:22

The noise of this world constantly blares in your ears. The Enemy has surrounded you with things you're told you need to possess, lifestyles you deserve to experience, and behaviors that guarantee fun and excitement—all are the ensnaring deceits of worldly riches. The workplace makes false promises too—job security, prestige, easy income and can't-lose investments.

The delusion created by worldly wealth is so effective and the attachment to material things is so strong, it's no wonder Jesus said, *"It is easier for a camel to go through the eye of a needle than for a rich man to enter the kingdom of God"* (Matthew 19:24). God's children are clearly not immune to this deception either. Far too often when those glittering enticements appear, believers simply reach for them without thinking. A few will even ask God to bless what they've already decided to do, rather like nonbelievers rubbing a rabbit's foot or checking their horoscopes for favorable conditions. Many believers just pursue the things of the world with the same focus and energy as nonbelievers, thinking the attainment of material comforts will be their indication that God really loves them and is answering their prayers by providing everything on their wish lists. To the contrary, wealth and material comforts can actually become deadly snares if they cause us to settle down and stop our pursuit of God and His purposes for our lives. That's perhaps why John Wesley made this emphatic statement:

"The deceitfulness of riches—deceitful indeed! They put out the eyes, harden the heart, steal away all the life of God, fill the soul with pride, anger, love of the world and make men enemies of the whole cross of Christ! Yet all the while they are eagerly desired, and vehemently pursued, even by those who believe there is a God!"[7] It takes real spiritual maturity to receive material riches and not be derailed by them.

You also need to know that Kingdom citizenship does not guarantee a comfortable life. It promises a meaningful one that extends from now into eternity. Furthermore, it is only the blessing of the Lord that can make you rich without added sorrow (Proverbs 10:22). If you know that God alone is in the best position to determine whether that "too-good-to-be-true" something is a blessing or a snare…

SPEAK IT OUT:

· I will not trust the riches or promises of this world for my happiness or future.

· By faith I accept the leading of the Holy Spirit to keep me from the snares of the Enemy.

· The Word of God is precious to me. I will not be distracted by the counterfeit when I have God's Truth.

WALK IT OUT:

Blessings that aren't! Can you reflect on a time when you got what you asked for and were sorry that you did? It can be as simple as a time when you were allowed to eat sweets to your heart's content only to experience the stomachache of all time after you had indulged. Or perhaps you've experienced the huge heartbreak of a big business deal that turns into a financial disaster.

---

[7] John Wesley, "Parable of the Sower," from *The Essential Works of John Wesley*, Barbour Publishing, Ulrichsville, OH, 2011, p. 774.

Now, was there a time when you waited to hear from God and moved forward in His peace? Which result do you prefer? Doesn't the fact that God created you, your design and your destiny qualify Him alone to direct your life?

My Journal Notes

DAY DEEPLY ROOTED

*"But the one who received the seed that fell on good soil is
the man who hears the word and understands it.
He who produces a crop, yielding a hundred, sixty or
thirty times what was sown."*

- MATTHEW 13:23

This verse is a particular favorite of "prosperity gospel" proponents. They use it to claim that God promises to return every seed planted—from watches and automobiles to money and land—with more of the same in great abundance, whenever that seed is planted (given away) in faith. Don't believe it. As we've already seen, the incorruptible seed referred to in this parable is the Word of God and the good soil is the heart of someone who treasures what the Word promises and is positioned to respond to the Lord's instruction in obedience. It is God who decides when the seed will produce its harvest and how great that harvest will be. The supposed secret law of attraction[8] has nothing to do with it. Fruit produced by the incorruptible seed will bless others and further the Kingdom of God. There is nothing in the character or life of Jesus Christ to suggest that God's Word can be used as a personal wealth-building strategy.

At the same time know that the Word never fails to produce. When God instructed Isaac to plant in a time of famine, he did so in obedience and God brought forth a hundredfold return (Genesis 26). That harvest was the

---

[8] Law of attraction—a new age term used to describe the phenomena of "like attracting like." It borrows from the biblical law of "as you sow, so shall you reap" but fails to acknowledge God as the source of this spiritual principle. It stands in opposition to the Word in claiming that the individual is solely responsible for bringing circumstances into his life.

product of God's specific word of instruction and Isaac's faithful obedience, nothing else. God's Word will not return to Him void, but will accomplish that which it was sent forth to accomplish, by His grace. Your part is to prepare your heart through time in God's presence and obedience to His will. Remember that as you seek the Kingdom, God will add everything else, so...

SPEAK IT OUT:

· I am determined to give God's Word good soil to grow in. I make His Word a priority in my life.

· I invite the Holy Spirit to help me focus on and understand God's living word for my life.

· By faith I am one who will produce high yield crops and great fruit in my life for the Kingdom.

WALK IT OUT:

Health Food: We are reflections of our diet, spiritually and physically. Put junk food in on a consistent basis and you're likely to develop health problems. Fill yourself with a steady diet of media and world messaging, and spiritual disease is sure to manifest as well. So what are you eating: the Bread of Life found in God's Word or the world's buffet of artificial life sweeteners served with hefty portions of doom and gloom? Keep track of the messages you attend to today. Make a record of the time spent watching television, reading the newspaper, listening to the radio and ingesting messages of the world. Now compare that amount of time with the actual time spent listening to, discussing, reading and ingesting messages of God's Kingdom. Based on the balance of your spiritual diet, how healthy should you expect to be?

My Journal Notes

WEEK 3

KINGDOM FIRST

"But seek first his kingdom and his righteousness, and all these things will be given to you as well."

- MATTHEW 6:33

There's no trick to this scripture. It's a clear as it can be. If you give the pursuit of God first place in your life, He will provide you with absolutely everything you need. Without a doubt, this is the most radical—and the most important—direction you will ever receive. God's personal instruction for you this day, whether you are searching for your next work assignment or trying to decide what to do about your current situation, is to seek the Kingdom of God above every other thing. And He means it! So make it your top priority to learn all you can about the King and His Kingdom, its laws and customs, and your place in it as quickly as you can. Don't excuse yourself by saying you don't have time to give God's Word any attention right now given your employment situation. The command is do this *first!*

If you're confused about where to begin, you'll find your starting place this week. You'll learn about Kingdom culture and timing through the teachings of Jesus and then spend some time gaining an understanding of

Christ's righteousness. In His righteousness you'll be given the keys to God's Kingdom. Along the way, you'll also learn about the very heart and character of your new Employer, Almighty God, as embodied by His Son, Jesus. Your final weekly objective will be to better understand the "family business" that you've been adopted into and to begin to see your proper place.

You may be hesitating at the idea of joining the Company of God's true saints, perhaps thinking you won't like it. Don't buy the lie that the world kingdom has more to offer you. C.S. Lewis describes life outside God's plan like this: "When we want to be something other than the thing God wants us to be, we must be wanting what, in fact, will not make us happy."[9] There simply is no greater joy or happiness than that found in Kingdom life. When you surrender your work and career to Jesus, He will guide your steps, lead you to opportunities you can't find on your own, and open doors that won't open by any other means. The Bible even tells us that God is the One behind every promotion.

What a shame it is that most people, including believers, spend all their time and energy trying to take care of their basic needs by themselves when God has proven Himself to be the far better and more generous Provider. In His will you'll find both meaning and satisfaction. If you're ready to claim the abundant life God has prepared for you…

 ## SPEAK IT OUT:

· I am a citizen in the Kingdom of God.

· I live by the laws of His Kingdom and I serve His will and purposes only.

· I choose to live in the fear of the Lord and to seek wisdom at all costs.

---

[9] C.S. Lewis, *The Problem of Pain*, New York, NY, Macmillan, 1962, p. 52.

My Journal Notes

DAY 1   KINGDOM CULTURE

"What is the kingdom of God like? What shall I compare it to? It is like a mustard seed, which a man took and planted in his garden. It grew and became a tree, and the birds of the air perched in its branches."

- LUKE 13:18-19

The Kingdom of God that Jesus spoke about was really a mystery to the people of His day. They expected a warrior King to arrive and deliver them, just as God had done in the past. In your work circumstances you might also be hoping for some immediate and dramatic rescue. Certainly that might be God's response to your specific need, but it's more likely you'll experience the Kingdom of God in accordance with the following:

First and most importantly, you'll discover this Kingdom is the *true* good news (Luke 4:44). All the world's riches, comforts, temptations and happiness pale in comparison to the lasting, authentic and very real benefits of the Kingdom of God. And, while its origin and roots are in the spirit realm, it provides God's "employees" with both spiritual and material blessings in this realm. Don't let anyone tell you God isn't practical or that His blessings are never tangible.

Second, God's Kingdom is invisible, but its impact is not (Luke 13:40). Like yeast in flour, the spiritual working of God's Kingdom changes the nature of everything it encounters. You will experience the Spirit in you—sanctifying, healing and transforming your life. Through you, the Kingdom will transform the workplace and bring more souls to salvation.

Finally, the real work of the Kingdom will be accomplished by God, not you. *"Therefore, my beloved, as you have always obeyed, not as in my presence only, but now much more in my absence, work out your own salvation with fear and trembling; for it is God who works in you both to will and to do for His good pleasure"* (Philippians 2:12-13). It's not up to you to decide where or how to plant the seeds of the Kingdom, nor do you have to force anything to happen. God will grow His seeds in your life if you will simply show up each day and follow His instructions. If you're ready for the true "experience of a lifetime"...

SPEAK IT OUT:

· By faith I know that the Kingdom of God is alive and growing in me now.

· As a citizen of God's Kingdom, I am the salt that preserves and gives flavor to my world.

· The light of God's Kingdom shines through me, and I bring Him glory.

WALK IT OUT:

Reflections: Reflect on the events of your life. Can you remember times when the Lord did something wonderful for you? Have you witnessed His healing, provision, direction or protection in your life or in the lives of those you love? Do you recall the day when you discovered His love for you and the joy of knowing your sins had been forgiven? Can you tell the Bible stories that recount His love for every person who sought after Him? Praise Him today. Tell Him how much you love Him. Then go out and find someone to whom you can tell the Good News of Jesus Christ. Take some time, while inside or outside the workplace, to spread the Gospel of Jesus Christ.

My Journal Notes

KINGDOM TIMING

"The coming of the kingdom of God does not come with your careful observation, nor will people say, 'Here it is,' or 'There it is,' because the kingdom of God is within you."

- LUKE 17:20

The experience of time—past, present, and future—poses a great deal of difficulty for most believers. It is impossible for the human mind to really grasp that God stands outside of time, in eternity. This means that He is observing what you are doing right now and He is observing right now what you are doing tomorrow and every other day in the future as well. Because of His unique position, God has already seen the end of your life from before the beginning and nothing about you or your circumstances will ever surprise Him. Do you understand that this means He has already seen every twist and turn in your work life and has prepared provisions and good plans to address every one? (Jeremiah 29:11)

There will never be a time when you are too late with your prayers or your repentance. You may just discover your sin, mistake or need today, but God saw you reaching this point before you were born so He's already standing in your future with your solution!

The timing of the Kingdom is equally mysterious—it is already here and yet it is also coming in the future. You can go to work every day knowing that the all-powerful Holy Spirit already resides in you, to help you accomplish the great things to which you are called. Keep your eyes open and you'll see that the Kingdom and the love of Christ are already working through you.

You can also look forward to the day when King Jesus will return. If it's your desire that He find you faithfully working as a good steward on that day…

 ## Speak it out:

- I am a citizen of God's Kingdom, which has no end. That Kingdom is growing within me now.

- By faith I trust the indwelling Spirit of God to lead me to my destiny in Christ.

- I thank God for the privilege of being His child and a participant in the birth of His Kingdom on Earth.

 ## Walk it out:

Try, try again: The world's timing is never permanent. Sometimes opportunities exist right under our noses that weren't there a minute ago. Everything is changing all the time. For example, don't assume that a position that was filled 90 days ago is no longer available. Many employers have a 90-day probation for new employees and are quick to release people who don't meet their expectations. It's also not unusual for job seekers to accept a job only to receive a second offer and leave for something better. So, go back to past recruitment ads, find those filled 90 days ago, and call to see if they might be open again. You just might be the first one through the door on the second round of hiring. God alone is unchanging, all other situations must yield under His mighty hand.

My Journal Notes

DAY **WHOSE RIGHTEOUSNESS?**

"But seek first his kingdom and his righteousness,
and all these things will be given to you as well."

- MATTHEW 6:33

Let's revisit a scripture we've looked at before because there's a point here that many miss. Jesus directs us to seek *His* righteousness. It does not say, "Seek first the Kingdom and then try to make yourself righteous." You cannot clean yourself up enough to become acceptable to God. You just need to fully understand the gift you received from Jesus when He gave you His righteousness as an overwhelming act of His grace. It is Christ's righteousness, not yours, that opens the Kingdom to you! Your faith in Jesus accomplishes miraculous things, NOT faith in yourself. You can bring nothing to this privileged employment status except your acceptance, gratitude and obedience.

If you keep trying to trust in yourself and your good works, you'll never conquer the problems of the workplace. When your problems remain despite your best efforts and prayers, don't say, "I must not have enough faith." God has given you an adequate measure of faith to do the job. And don't claim that you must not be in right standing with God, because you are standing in the righteousness of Jesus. It is by the finished work of Jesus that you can boldly approach God to get your needs met. Jesus is the One who got you *hired* into your Kingdom assignment, remember? Count on Him and you'll be fine.

There are reasons for prayers to appear unanswered, but your acceptability to God is not among them. You were made fully acceptable by Jesus. If, on the other hand, sin is blocking you from *accepting* His grace and mercy, repent and ask the Holy Spirit to remove it from your life. Whenever God looks at you, He sees you through the blood of Jesus and judges you as righteous and worthy. Accept that and keep your eyes on Jesus. Now...

SPEAK IT OUT:

- I believe in the finished work of Jesus Christ that conquered sin and death.

- By faith I accept that I have received the free gift of His righteousness and have been brought into right standing with God.

- I surrender all that I am to the sanctifying work of the Holy Spirit within.

WALK IT OUT:

Tell Me About Yourself: This question is asked countless times by strangers, dates, interviewers and network contacts—but, guess what? They don't really want to know all that much about you. They just want to know enough to decide if you are what they might be interested in, now or in the future. If you don't have an honest answer that will help them settle the matter in their minds, you lose. Take the time to prepare and rehearse your response until you can accomplish the following four objectives while coming across as natural and sincere:

1. Tell the listener how you will organize and present the information about yourself.

2. Maintain eye contact and an open, friendly posture.

3. Include specific results and contributions you've made to a prior employer.

4. Wrap up with a future objective that includes making a contribution to any organization you join.

My Journal Notes

DAY 4   **MEET YOUR EMPLOYER—GOD**

"If you, then, though you are evil, know how to give good gifts to your children, how much more will your Father in heaven give good gifts to those who ask him!"

- MATTHEW 7:11

As Moses stood on the banks of the Jordan River, he said to God, *"You have only begun to show your greatness and the strength of your hand"* (Deuteronomy 3:24 NLT). If that was just the beginning, can you imagine the full scope of God's love? God had already delivered, protected and guided His people for forty years. He had fed them continuously, provided water in the desert, and sheltered them. That statement by Moses, who knew God well, reveals that your Employer God can and does meet every practical need. He stands ready to extend that same strength and greatness to you, His employee. Jesus wants you to know this about your Father today!

Take some time to get to know God and you'll discover that He is caring and ever-present. Study what Jesus teaches about Him until you come to trust in His perfect love for you. Realize that Jesus, in His life and ministry, demonstrated the Father's heart for you. Become fully persuaded that God desires to heal, deliver, feed, sustain and protect you. He seeks a personal relationship with you so He can share His love and bring you into His perfect plan for your life.

He is God in three Persons. You'll encounter Him in all His divine forms this week, but today—see Him as Father, Creator and Almighty God, with the power, eternal perspective, and desire to deal with all your challenges and lead you in triumph over them all. He is love, and His love for you knows no bounds. If you know He's completely trustworthy and that He loves you unconditionally…

SPEAK IT OUT:

· I trust my Creator with my life.

· I know that God is ever near me and I feel the presence of His Spirit within me.

· My heart is to seek and follow God, who is all powerful, all sufficient and perfect Love.

WALK IT OUT:

Put off Childish Things: Do you believe in Santa Claus, fairies, or leprechauns? Even if you once believed in them, now that you are older these imaginary beings no longer prompt you to search for a pot of gold at the rainbow's end or rush out Christmas morning in search of a full stocking from Santa, do they?

Now that you have been saved by Jesus, do you still think you're on your own to solve your work problems? Are you still acting as if God lacks the provisions you need or has decided to withhold them so you alone must provide for your family? Catch yourself whenever you find your beliefs contradicting what Jesus says. Today, identify one belief you're holding about Him that suggests He is unloving, uncaring, or unable to help you. If you cannot back up your belief with Scripture, change your mind about it. Remember this, "Faith is not the belief that God will do what you want. It is the belief that God will do what is right."[10]

---

[10] Max Lucado, "He Still Moves Stones," *The Lucado Inspirational Reader*, Thomas Nelson, Nashville, TN, 2011, p. 133.

My Journal Notes

DAY 5 — WORKING FOR YOUR FATHER

"Don't you believe that I am in the Father, and that the Father is in me? The words I say to you are just not my own. Rather, it is the Father, living in me, who is doing his work."

- JOHN 14:10

Before we explore today's scripture, it's important to draw attention to a foundational truth about your relationship with this Employer. First and foremost, He is your Father and you are His adopted child. No matter what you may have experienced with your earthly father, God has revealed the perfect standard of fatherhood in His relationship with Jesus. And just as He related to Jesus, so He desires to relate to you. "In, through and under Jesus Christ their Lord they (believers) are ruled, loved, companied with and honored by their heavenly Father." [11]

As for the nature of your work with the Father—Jesus offers this extraordinary insight. He tells us He did not work, or even speak, on His own. He was simply demonstrating a completely yielded life that allowed the Father to work through Him. If Jesus wouldn't take action without God, why would you?

You ought to find great relief in this teaching. It turns out that everything doesn't depend on you! God isn't watching you to see if you can figure out your problems and get it right. According to Jesus, here's how it works: *"He who has My commandments and keeps them, it is he who loves Me. And he who loves Me will be loved by My Father, and I will love him and manifest Myself to him"* (John 14:21).

---

[11] J.I. Packer, *Knowing God*, InterVarsity Press, Downers Grove, IL, 1993, p. 205.

Your part is to seek Him and bring Him your questions. His part is to tell you how to handle them. Can you imagine a partnership as wonderful as that? No wonder Jesus teaches that His yoke is easy. If you like the way the Father worked through Jesus, don't you think it would be great to have Him calling the shots in your life too?

Lose the idea that God is some kind of disapproving taskmaster to be avoided at all costs. He is the mercy, wisdom, power and love you see demonstrated in Jesus. Honor Jesus' commands, and He and the Father will come through just for you. If you agree that there's nothing in the workplace that can't be handled in this business partnership ...

 SPEAK IT OUT:

· I work for my Father and He is the King over all things.

· I am a royal child and my provision is assured.

· I have the power and authority of the name of Jesus to use as I serve Him.

 WALK IT OUT:

That's Impossible: What job search activity or work assignment seems impossible to you? Do you struggle to make phone calls to strangers, speak publicly, or complete applications online? Maybe you freeze up in interviews and business presentations. We all have our struggles. Have you asked God for His strategy to deal with yours?

Today tell God about your most difficult workplace challenge. Ask for the power of the Holy Spirit and the mind of Christ to help you master it. Don't think for a minute that God isn't interested and willing to help. He is faithful to do in you and through you what you cannot do on your own.

My Journal Notes

WEEK 4

KINGDOM RESOURCES

"You have heard,... 'Do not not murder...But I tell you that anyone who is angry with his brother will be subject to judgment....
You have heard,... 'Do not commit adultery.'
But I tell you that anyone who looks at a woman lustfully has already committed adultery with her in his heart.
Again, you have heard,... 'Do not break your oath'...But I tell you, do not swear at all....
You have heard,... 'Eye for eye, and tooth for tooth.'
But I tell you, Do not resist an evil person.
If anyone strikes you on the right cheek, turn to him the other cheek also....
You have heard,... 'Love your neighbor and hate your enemy.' But I tell you: Love your enemies and pray for those who persecute you, that you may be sons of your Father in heaven."

- MATTHEW 5:21-45

As you read today's scripture, it should be obvious that Jesus was bringing the world a major course correction in its understanding of God. Clearly, Jesus was trying to switch attention from man's outward behaviors to the inward condition of his heart. Today He is still trying to shift your priorities. This week you'll learn about the resources God has provided to help you make this critical transition.

Most employers provide orientation resources to help new employees become successful. Their goal is to reduce the new associates' learning curve and make them productive as quickly as possible. To assist you with this learning experience, God is providing the following:

- **The perfect supervisor** (and you can take that term literally). Jesus Christ will not only teach you about the Kingdom and how it works, but you'll see Him in action. He'll be your role model. He will demand your obedience because that's how He can ensure your safety and blessing.

- **The perfect trainer.** Jesus said His return to Heaven would be to your advantage, for it would make way for the indwelling Holy Spirit. You can now speak to your God, in the Spirit, every time you bow your head and whisper to your heart.

- **The perfect employee handbook.** Containing sixty-six books in one, this handbook, the Bible, may appear daunting, but there is no expectation that you will master its contents in this 90-day period, or even your lifetime. Here's a tip: You might want to start in the New Testament gospels (Matthew, Mark, Luke and John) to read in full context the scriptures highlighted each day. Make sure you invite your Trainer to read with you and to help you understand the message within the words.

- **The perfect "hotline."** You are now, and always will be, in open, continuous contact with God and Jesus through the Holy Spirit inside you. When you don't even know what to ask for or how to pray, the Spirit will take over at your invitation and speak for you in the perfect will of the Father.

If you understand that everything you need to know is now available to you...

 **SPEAK IT OUT:**

- Jesus is my Savior, Master and Lord. He reveals the heart and will of my Father for me.

- By faith I walk in the love of God as demonstrated by Jesus, the living Word of God.

- I trust the Holy Spirit to teach me the ways of the Kingdom that I might bring God glory.

My Journal Notes

DAY 1 — YOUR SUPERVISOR

*"Whoever serves me must follow me; and where
I am, my servant also will be.
My Father will honor the one who serves me."*

- JOHN 12:26

Kingdom work is hard work. Success in the Father's business will require you to master two very difficult behaviors—surrender and obedience—and only Jesus is qualified to teach this. So, with the Lord as your Supervisor you can expect this to be His emphasis. A tip to get you started—learn to wait on the Lord. Don't try to run out on your own and do great things for the Kingdom. You'll only undermine your faith and discredit the Word if you move without His direction. Following His lead and listening for His voice are two of the most important things you'll ever learn in support of surrender and obedience. Start now and let the workplace or job search in which you currently find yourself be your personal learning laboratory.

It's also obvious that Jesus wants you to have compassion for others—all others, including everyone you encounter in the workplace and all those with whom you work. The faster you learn to take yourself and your feelings out of the picture and keep your focus on serving them, the better you'll be. Jesus also places a high priority on your behavior in His family, with those who also aspire to be His disciples. His beloved apostle John says it this way: *"If someone says, 'I love God,' and hates his brother, he is a liar; for he who does not love his brother whom he has seen, how can he love God whom he has not seen?"* (1 John 4:20 NKJV). After all, your love for your brothers and sisters in Christ is how the world will know you are Christ's disciple.

One more thing—there will probably be days when you'll want to quit.

When that happens, remember Peter's response to Jesus' question: *"'You do not want to leave too, do you?' Jesus asked the Twelve. Simon Peter answered him, 'Lord, to whom shall we go? You have the words of eternal life. We believe and know that you are the Holy One of God'"* (John 6:67-69). "Jesus Christ is not another teacher; He is the final teacher and the last Word of God to men. What He has said closes all other arguments."[12] If you understand that Jesus is God and you desire to follow Him…

 ## Speak it out:

· My house is built on the Rock, Jesus Christ, and I am secure.

· I hear Jesus' commands and I do them. I know that obedience keeps me safe from harm.

· By faith I trust in God through every storm and listen for His voice to direct my steps.

 ## Walk it out:

Follow the Leader: How strong is your self-control? Can you rein yourself in and willingly let someone else take the lead? Surrender is the indication of true self-management. How good have you been at taking orders without resentment and willingly following directions in your prior jobs? It's great to be a star racehorse, but if you can't be broken, if you refuse to wear a saddle, you just may be a talent that cannot be used in the workplace. To get into the harness with Jesus, you must be able to submit to authority. Find an opportunity today to allow someone else to take the lead and watch yourself to see how well you follow.

---

[12] A.W. Tozer, *Experiencing the Presence of God*, Regal, Ventura, CA, 2010, p. 32.

My Journal Notes

DAY 2 — YOUR ROLE MODEL AND MENTOR

"Take my yoke upon you and learn from me,
for I am gentle and humble in heart,
and you will find rest for your souls."

- MATTHEW 11:29

Yesterday you saw Jesus in the role of your supervisor. Today you'll see that He is also your role model and mentor. "Jesus knows how you feel. You're under the gun at work? Jesus knows how you feel. You've got more to do than is humanly possible? So did he. People take more from you than they give? Jesus understands…You are precious to him. So precious that he became like you so you would come to him."[13] He has walked in your shoes and understands what you're up against. He's "been there and done that" and now He wants to help you through all your challenges. The secret Jesus knew is that a life of perfect love requires the supernatural empowerment of God. He knew how to get out of God's way and allow the Father to work through Him. You'll need to learn to do this too, and to let the love of Christ work through you.

But right now, notice how Jesus responded to people in their times of failing and weakness. When Peter began to sink into the choppy water, Jesus grabbed him and put him back in the boat (Matthew 14:30). When a skeptical father struggled with unbelief, Jesus had compassion for him and healed his son (Mark 9:24). The point is that you don't have to "measure up" to get the undivided attention and compassion of Jesus. He will never leave or forsake you, never fail to calm the storms or help you when you cry out to him (Mark 4:39).

---

[13] Max Lucado, "In the Eye of the Storm," *The Lucado Inspirational Reader*, Thomas Nelson, Nashville, TN, 2011, pp. 99-101.

Learn to put your complete trust in His love for you. Know that when you need His help, He will always be willing to give it and…

Speak it out:

· Jesus loves me, this I know. He will never fail to rescue me.

· I have a Savior who understands me and is always interceding on my behalf.

· By faith I trust in the finished work of Jesus at Calvary. I rest in Him.

Walk it out:

Take a Break: *"Remember the Sabbath day, to keep it holy. Six days you shall labor and do all your work, but the seventh day is the Sabbath of the LORD your God"* (Exodus 20:8-19 NKJV). Somehow this commandment seems to have gotten completely lost today. Jesus stated, *"The Sabbath was made for man, not man for the Sabbath"* (Mark 2:27), and that was all it took for believers to stop treating the Sabbath as anything other than a non-work day that they could spend any way that they please. Jesus fully observed the spirit of this commandment, and it applies to you today.

Have you ever considered why God might be calling you into this weekly time with Him? It isn't because He needs a day of worship, for He needs nothing. No, this day was given for your sake. You need a full day of separateness from the world and workplace in order to stay centered and renewed in Him. Because Jesus is the Lord of the Sabbath and has promised to give rest to anyone who comes to Him, ask Him to draw you into one dedicated day of rest and worship in His presence each week.

My Journal Notes

DAY **YOUR TRAINER**

"But the Helper, the Holy Spirit, whom the Father will send in My name, He will teach you all things, and bring to your remembrance all things that I said to you."

- JOHN 14:26 NKJV

If you cooperate, the Holy Spirit will train you to behave supernaturally. By God's grace and the gift of His Spirit, you can *"be clothed with power from on high"* (Luke 24:49) and learn to live every moment of your life in the power, authority and love of Jesus Christ as you willingly surrender yourself to His perfect will. You won't decide when and how to use the power of God—even Jesus did not presume to do that. He waited to see what the Father would do before He acted and so must you (John 5:19).

It's important to know that you can grieve the Holy Spirit by ignoring His voice and choosing to disobey His direction (Ephesians 4:30-31). He lives inside you to empower you to act on behalf of Jesus Christ in the workplace and the world. You are not to ignore Him any more than you would Jesus if He showed up physically to work with you today!

With your ear tuned to the Spirit, you will represent the Kingdom *to the glory of God.* He will reveal your identity in Christ and what God has in mind for you. As you go through your workday, He'll remind you about what Jesus has taught and empower you to walk in love. *"But you, dear friends, by building yourselves up in your most holy faith and praying in the Holy Spirit, keep yourselves in God's love as you wait for the mercy of our Lord Jesus Christ to bring you to eternal life"* (Jude 2:20-21). Thank God you've been given an indwelling Helper so that you can successfully fulfill your mission as a citizen of His Kingdom. Your sole responsibility is to show up for training every morning, suited up and ready to learn. If you're ready to let the training begin…

SPEAK IT OUT:

- I receive the Holy Spirit as my Helper, Teacher and Guide. I work with supernatural empowerment.

- By study and training in God's Word, I learn to recognize the voice of the Holy Spirit.

- I expect to receive life-changing insights that the world doesn't possess.

WALK IT OUT:

Broken Resolutions: Are you a person who makes New Year's resolutions? If so, have you ever failed to break a bothersome old bad habit or stick to the new one you resolved to adopt at the start of a new year? It's frustrating when you can't get control of yourself and your behaviors, but often it's because you are trying to work from the outside in.

Realize that the things you say and do are the products of your beliefs and thoughts. Allow God to convict you of the root causes of your behavior problems. Then ask the Spirit to change you. Be open to discovering which of your behaviors, words and thoughts are not in the character of Jesus Christ. Surrender your heart to the sanctifying power of the Holy Spirit. Be transformed by God's Word! Focus on this today and identify at least one inside-out work God wants to do in you.

My Journal Notes

DAY **THE ORIGINAL EMPLOYEE HANDBOOK**

"Do not think that I have come to abolish the Law or the Prophets; I have not come to abolish them but to fulfill them. I tell you the truth, until heaven and earth disappear, not the smallest letter, not the least stroke of a pen, will by any means disappear from the Law until everything is accomplished."

- MATTHEW 5:17-18

In the Bible, you have been given the most awesome employee handbook ever created. Every bit of it *"is God-breathed and is useful for teaching, rebuking, correcting and training in righteousness"* (2 Timothy 3:16). A.W. Tozer describes the uniqueness of your Heavenly handbook this way: *"God did not write a book and send it by messenger to be read at a distance by unaided minds. He spoke a Book and lives in His spoken words, constantly speaking His words and causing the power of them to persist across the years."* [14] Can you comprehend this? Each time you pick it up and dive in, you encounter Almighty God and can actually learn to hear His voice behind the words.

In the workplace employees are frequently given employee handbooks that they may never read. Don't let that describe you with this Handbook. Don't wait for a crisis to send you scrambling to it, frantic for answers. Long before His ministry actually began Jesus was studying and discussing the truths contained in the Scriptures (Luke 2:46). If He considered it necessary, shouldn't you?

If you have tried to read the Word but have never been able to stick

---

[14] A.W. Tozer, *The Pursuit of God*, Wing Spread Publishers, Camp Hill, PA, 1982, p. 75.

with it or understand it, realize that you cannot receive God's Word with an *unaided mind*. Invite the Holy Spirit to give you understanding as you read. Ask Jesus to increase your hunger and thirst for His Word. Approach the Bible as your personal source of wisdom, and study it by topics of importance to you. Feed your spirit with the Word of God as diligently as you feed your body. Go into the workforce *"strong in the Lord and in the power of His might"* (Ephesians 6:10 NKJV) and...

Speak it out:

· I believe in the power of the Word of God and give it place in my life each day.

· By faith I accept that Jesus, the living Word, still speaks to me through the Bible and I find answers there.

· Everything I need to know about my work, purpose and life can be found in God's Word.

Walk it out:

I'm Ready: When are you most alert and ready to learn? Set aside that time to study the Word of God. Don't wait until you're nodding off to sleep or try to concentrate before you're fully awake. In other words, don't give the Word a scrap of your day or a "hand-me-down" of time when you're not at your best. Study His Word as if your life depends on it, because it does! Don't try to cover a book a day. You can begin by just pulling out a single meaningful verse, ponder it, memorize it and ask for revelation about how to apply it to your life. This is your daily bread, so eat up!

My Journal Notes

DAY **EVERYTHING YOU NEED TO KNOW**

"It is the Spirit who gives life; the flesh profits nothing. The words that I speak to you are spirit, and they are life."

- JOHN 6:63 NKJV

Many organizations have Help Desks and Employee Assistance Programs to support their employees on the job. God has gone far beyond this. He has taken all His power and authority and placed it in Jesus to be made available to His employees through the Holy Spirit whenever it is needed! *"All that belongs to the Father is mine. That is why I said the Spirit will take from what is mine and make known to you"* (John 16:15).

Imagine that! Everything you will ever need in order to accomplish your work is available to you 24/7. You can access the mind of Christ and gain wisdom to help you with any employment or business decision at any time, day or night.

Paul explains this amazing, life-giving resource in this way: *"Now we have received, not the spirit of the world, but the Spirit who is from God, that we might know the things that have been freely given to us by God. These things we also speak, not in words which man's wisdom teaches but which the Holy Spirit teaches, comparing spiritual things with spiritual. But the natural man does not receive the things of the Spirit of God, for they are foolishness to him; nor can he know them, because they are spiritually discerned"* (1 Corinthians 2:12-14 NLT).

But oh, what amazing gifts we have been given in each and every promise of God. Charles Spurgeon eloquently stated it this way: "No promise is of private interpretation. Whatever God has said to any one saint, he has said to all. When he opens a well for one, it is that all may drink. When he opens a granary-door to give out food, there may be some one starving man who is the occasion of its being opened, but all hungry saints may come and feed too." [15] Take the time, beginning today, to look up every reference that contains the words "in Christ, through Christ, by Christ, in Him, through Him and by Him." Write down every statement that tells you about your spiritual *identity in Christ*—who you are, what you now have and what you can do. This is what Jesus purchased for you at the Cross. Now it's up to you to live it out by faith. Stay connected to your supernatural "Help Desk" to fully receive the spirit and life you have been given. If you're ready to become the person you're designed to be...

Speak it out:

- Jesus Christ is more than enough. The finished work of Calvary transforms my life now.

- I walk by faith and not by sight. My confidence is in the Kingdom of God.

- God's spiritual Kingdom meets all my practical needs and feeds both my body and my spirit.

Walk it out:

Mining Miracles: Today take a tour from Genesis to Revelation and capture the many miraculous stories of God's interventions on behalf of His children. Don't stop until you have at least a dozen. Compare the magnitude

---

[15] Charles Spurgeon, *Morning and Evening*, Hendrickson Publishers, Peabody, MA, 1995, p. 108.

of God's actions with the smallness of man's needs. If God can make the sun stand still in the sky and split the Red Sea wide open, how difficult do you think it will be for God to provide you with opportunities, create openings or bring your skills to life in a new work assignment?

My Journal Notes

KINGDOM JOB DESCRIPTION

"The work of God is this: to believe in the one he has sent."

- JOHN 6:29

In the workplace traditional job descriptions include KSAs—descriptions of the Knowledge, Skills and Attributes required for successful performance. These become the requirements that guide the recruiting and selection of individuals to fill jobs.

In the Kingdom of God, the situation is completely the opposite. First you are "hired" and then God begins the process of building and developing the Knowledge, Skills and Attributes required for success in His Kingdom through the tasks He has planned for you. According to Jesus in today's scripture, you must satisfy only one requirement in order to qualify for Kingdom employment—believe in the One sent by God, Jesus.

This week you'll learn what God has in mind for you as preparation for performing your Kingdom job description. The following is a brief overview of the content you'll cover:

- **Knowledge:** Pretty much everything you now know will need to be changed. To the degree that you've been taught by the world, you can expect to discover that you're making decisions based on lies and error. Now you'll have to take every thought captive, examine it in light of the truth, and keep only those that align with the Word (2 Corinthians 10:5). The key to your transformed life is a renewed mind (Romans 12:2).

- **Skills:** Before you were born, God designed you to fulfill a divine destiny. You have skills and talents that were given for the express purpose of enabling you to accomplish that destiny. Your gifts may help you in the workplace (Proverbs 18:16), or they may enable you to bless others apart from your work. You simply need to discover what they are—the Holy Spirit will direct you in their use.

- **Attributes:** These are the personality traits that will best enable you to walk in the Spirit life of the Kingdom of God. Because they are the natural attributes of a child, you have them within your nature. Surfacing them and putting them back to use may prove a challenge, however.

- **Response:** You'll also see that there is really only one right response to make when you receive your Kingdom job description. Given that your Employer will be providing everything you require in order to succeed, that response should be obvious.

(continued on next page)

- **Assignments:** The Kingdom tasks assigned to you may be a surprise. If you're expecting your initial assignments to be great spiritual endeavors, you're going to be disappointed. First you'll have to demonstrate faithful service with the little responsibilities you are given.

If you are interested in seeing your job description and willing to do whatever God assigns…

 ## SPEAK IT OUT:

· My mind is renewed and my life transformed by the Word of life, Jesus.

· In faith I receive the guidance, development and assignments God has prepared to make me into the image of Christ.

· I believe in Jesus Christ, the Son of God, and desire to know Him more and more.

My Journal Notes

DAY   KNOWLEDGE REQUIREMENTS

"And no one pours new wine into old wineskins. If he does, the wine will burst the skins, and both the wine and the wineskins will be ruined. No, he pours new wine into new wineskins."

– MARK 2:22

God's will for you is good and pleasing and perfect. Do you believe it? Or do you still want your way, your will and God's willingness to perform for you? Like so many others, you may think you know what would be best for you, so you're focusing all your energies on trying to get God to deliver on your demands. This behavior may be recommended by New Agers and prosperity gospel proponents, but Jesus clearly tells you to change your mind about this. You need a radically new way of thinking if you hope to participate in the Kingdom way of life.

When you first come into God's Kingdom, your mind is filled with human reasoning, false beliefs and arguments against God's Word. The apostle Paul draws the clear distinction between our very best, present day knowledge and God's: *"Now we see things imperfectly, like puzzling reflections in a mirror, but then we will see everything with perfect clarity. All that I know now is partial and incomplete, but then I will know everything completely, just as God now knows me completely"* (1 Corinthians 13:12 NLT). Given this, in whose knowledge do you choose to put your trust?

You may have also been taught that submission to the will of another must be resisted at all costs. For the sake of your divine destiny you will need to clean the house of your thoughts. The Enemy and the world have planted lies in your mind using the media, the workplace and unfortunately even the Church. You've probably been programmed to stay in control and be in charge. If you continue to think like the world, you'll defeat yourself by worrying, scheming, fretting and striving. So recognize this tactic and change your mind. *"Do not conform any longer to the pattern of this world, but be transformed by the renewing of your mind. Then you will be able to test and approve what God's will is—his good, pleasing and perfect will"* (Romans 12:2). If your mind is a new wineskin ready to receive what Jesus is pouring out for you...

SPEAK IT OUT:

· By faith I surrender my mind—all the false beliefs and errors in my thinking. I'm ready for new wineskins.

· My mind is renewed by the Word, and my life is transformed.

· I will not help the Enemy defeat me with my own wrong thinking.

WALK IT OUT:

Old Wineskins: *"And no one after drinking old wine wants the new, for he says, 'The old is better'"* (Luke 5:39). Every significant change, good or bad, will cause a strong, emotional reaction. When you experience change, it's human nature to focus on what you've lost, what you don't have, and what you can no longer do. To avoid the discomfort of transition, you might want to remain in "the comfort zone." Don't be led by your emotions, they'll deceive you every time. Just accept the discomfort of change as a temporary thing and keep your eyes on the prize of abundant life in Jesus.

My Journal Notes

DAY 2 SKILL REQUIREMENTS

"Neither do I condemn you; go and sin no more...
I am the light of the world. He who follows Me
shall not walk in darkness, but have the light of life."

- JOHN 8:11-12 NKJV

It's an often repeated statement that "God loves you just the way you are but He refuses to leave you that way." And although this is a common sermon topic, it's still a difficult concept to grasp. We wonder how God can love us completely when there is still so much wrong with us. It might help to realize that you started out as the perfect creation of a perfect God, and you have within you everything God needs to make you into the image of Christ. God knew you in your mother's womb and established plans and a destiny for you before you were ever born. His entire focus is on achieving that wonderful end outcome, in fellowship with you. All the events of life that have affected and changed you and all the choices you have made, good and bad, can't change God's heart towards you.

A.W. Tozer put it this way: "When our Lord looked at us, He saw not only what we were—He was faithful in seeing what we could become! He took away the curse of being and gave us the glorious blessing of becoming."[16] It's time to accept God's view and forget whatever self-image you may hold based on what the world has said about you. In Jesus you are not condemned, nor are you bound to the habits, sins or mistakes of your past. Now is the time to discover what you're good at, what you enjoy doing and what gives you joy. If you desire to discover the things that will point you

---

[16] A.W. Tozer, *Who Put Jesus on the Cross?*, Christian Publications, Camp Hill, PA, 1976, p. 166.

toward your true design and lead you to making your greatest contribution in the workplace and in the Body of Christ...

SPEAK IT OUT:

· I respond like the disciples and follow the Master wherever He leads.

· By faith I trust that God has wonderful plans for me. My Father loves me perfectly.

· I thank God for the skills, gifts and talents He has given me, and I dedicate them to His service.

WALK IT OUT:

Take a Hint: God designed you with your destiny in mind and equipped you with all you need. He desires for you to experience joy and satisfaction in your service to others. This is a great time to identify the work that brings you joy and satisfaction as He intended. Draw two columns on a sheet of paper. Label one LIKES and the other DISLIKES. Review your prior work experiences. What tasks, activities and workplace assignments were your favorites and which ones would you like to avoid in the future? Put them into the appropriate column and look at your lists. What do your "likes" have in common? Are you most effective when working with people or, perhaps, with details? Are you more productive when you work alone to accomplish tasks or as part of a team? The more you can learn about your design, the better and more accurately you'll be able to present yourself to employers and recognize the assignments "with your name on them."

My Journal Notes

DAY 3 ATTRIBUTE REQUIREMENTS

"Let the little children come to me, and do not hinder them, for the kingdom of God belongs to such as these. I tell you the truth, anyone who will not receive the kingdom of God like a little child will never enter it."

- MARK 10:14-15

What does it mean to "receive the kingdom of God like a little child"? Well, think about the attributes that first come to mind as you think about little children. Can you picture the way a child responds when promised a wonderful gift? That's one time when you will clearly see the attributes God is looking for in His employees—wonder, excitement, openness and trust. Just mention that a surprise is coming and a little one will start looking forward to it, trusting that it will be wonderful. Soon you'll hear the questions "Is it time yet? When will I get my present?" Hopeful anticipation starts before the gift is even opened. Then, whatever the gift, it is received with enthusiasm. Sometimes even the box and wrapping paper generate excitement! To a healthy and well-cared-for child, the future is always exciting and filled with wonder. Nothing appears frightening from the sheltering safety of a parent's arms.

This may not have been your childhood experience, however. Your parents or caregivers may never have given surprises just to delight you. Perhaps there were no gifts in your past. If you've never felt safe, it's difficult to trust that the future will be good or that God can be trusted. To the degree that you've been hurt by the world and the people in your life, you may really struggle to believe in the absolute, unconditional goodness and generosity of God. Don't worry. Jesus understands. He will be patient with you as you learn to receive His love and Kingdom like a little child.

Childlike trust, wonder, openness and excitement will grow in you if you stay focused on how much Jesus loves you. Don't worry about how much, or how well, you love Him right now. Just remember the price He paid for you at Calvary and how very much you are loved.

If you desire to trust in the safety of His arms and come to Him like a little child...

 **SPEAK IT OUT:**

· I know that I belong to God and that He loves me perfectly, just as I am.

· I receive by faith my eternal and abundant life, starting this very moment.

· I have a deep and personal relationship with the living Christ, my Savior. I trust Him.

 **WALK IT OUT:**

Little Things: Look around you today, wherever you are, and find a way to give the gift of kindness. Pay the receptionist a sincere compliment. Pray for a coworker struggling in a relationship with a teenager at home. Ask your boss what you can do to lend a hand in your department. Be simple and childlike in your desire to be helpful and spread happiness. Make a tiny difference in someone's life today.

My Journal Notes

DAY 4 — ONE RIGHT RESPONSE

"If they kept quiet, the stones along the road would burst into cheers!"

- LUKE 19:40 NLT

You've learned about the promises in God's Word, the gifts He's designed in you and the basic attributes that will help you walk into Kingdom life. Could God have made things any simpler? Pause a moment to think about what God has done for you. You have eternal life. Your sins are forgiven. The King, Almighty God, has adopted you and made you His heir! You have life now and the promise of a good future. If God never did another thing for you, wouldn't you still be blessed beyond measure?

It's really unfortunate that no one talks much about sin these days. Listen to the world's messages and you'll become convinced that God's forgiveness isn't that big a deal. Eternal life is treated like some insignificant fringe benefit—if it's mentioned at all. Don't allow this attitude in you! *"You did not give me a kiss, but this woman, from the time I entered, has not stopped kissing my feet. You did not put oil on my head, but she has poured perfume on my feet. Therefore, I tell you, her many sins have been forgiven—for she loved much. But he who has been forgiven little loves little"* (Luke 7:45-47). As you think about your response to God's goodness, are you more like the woman in this story or the ungrateful host?

Jesus Christ died for you. You owe Him your life. When He calls you, drop everything and follow. Keep thinking about what He's done for you and get carried away in gratitude! Become passionate about being a fisher of men and spreading the Good News of God's grace and salvation. Look around in your workplace and community to find ways to demonstrate His great love. Don't worry about "being cool" or fitting in. Be the hands and heart of Jesus.

"For I was hungry, and you fed me. I was thirsty, and you gave me a drink. I was a stranger, and you invited me into your home. I was naked, and you gave me clothing. I was sick, and you cared for me. I was in prison, and you visited me" (Matthew 25:35-36 NLT). Start now, right you are. Worship God with your life and...

 ## Speak it out:

- · I am so thankful for the gift of eternal life and freedom from the power of sin. The blessing of God is more than enough!

- · By faith I believe that my needs are met according to God's riches.

- · I thank God for Jesus, the most precious gift of love that the world has ever received.

 ## Walk it out:

Divine Thank You Notes: How about trying an experiment? Spend one whole day thanking God for every good thing big and small. Just reverse the all-too-common prayer habit of a quick thank you and a long laundry list of needs and disappointments. Instead, spend all your time thanking God for all He has already done, with a quick mention of the needs you're still waiting on in faith.

My Journal Notes

DAY 5   KINGDOM WORK ASSIGNMENTS

"The master was full of praise. 'Well done, my good and faithful servant. You have been faithful in handling this small amount, so now I will give you many more responsibilities. Let's celebrate together!'"

- MATTHEW 25:21 NLT

We all know the story here—a master gives a portion of his money to each of three servants and entrusts them to invest it for him while he is gone. In today's verse, Jesus tells you the master's response to the servant who successfully fulfilled his purpose. Notice how wonderful it will be to please the Master by faithfully managing whatever amount is entrusted to you. As a follower of Jesus you have been given an assignment—feed His sheep and demonstrate His love. You don't need to be a great evangelist or skilled preacher to do this. Love and bless the family, friends, work colleagues and fellow believers in your life. Be of service to those who don't know Jesus yet. Wait patiently and cheerfully as the Lord works out His plans on your behalf. Just be faithful with the opportunities you are given, and you will delight God!

Of course, you can bury the talent and skill you've been given, for fear of making a mistake. Using God's gifts requires taking risks. Many job seekers and workers struggle with choosing work assignments and making employment decisions, thinking they'll anger God with any misstep. As a result, they never move forward into the opportunities God places before them. If this has concerned you, relax. The greatest joy of a life surrendered to Christ is that He will use every situation and circumstance to the glory of God. Pursue the opportunities you choose, put your abilities to work with excellence and God will celebrate your choice with you!

Just remember, if you want to receive the Master's wages—prosperity, abundance and peace—you have to do your work the way He wants it done! If you're ready to go to work…

SPEAK IT OUT:

· Because of the love I have received, I desire to tell everyone about Jesus!

· By faith I receive wisdom and direction in order to use my gifts as God has designed.

· I celebrate with God as I bring Him a return on the love He has showered on me.

WALK IT OUT:

Busy Signals: There's an old saying that has its roots in the Jewish tradition, I believe. It warns us, "If the devil can't make you sin, he'll just make you busy." Where are you spending your time these days? Are you racing about but accomplishing little? Are you spending lots of time thinking about what you should or could be doing and relatively little time actually doing anything? In the craziness of your schedule, whatever it may include, are you ignoring people in order to accomplish tasks? Do you see how contrary that is to what Jesus teaches? Today set a personal goal to take time daily to settle down and plan in order to spend your time intentionally and productively—then do it! You know God's top priorities, so make sure they're top of your list too!

My Journal Notes

WEEK

PERFORMANCE EXPECTATIONS

"I am the vine; you are the branches. If a man remains in me and I in him, he will bear much fruit; apart from me you can do nothing."

- JOHN 15:5

This week you will review the expectations that God has for you as His employee. Just as Jesus offered the beatitudes in His Sermon on the Mount (Matthew 5), over the next five days you'll learn His "Be-attitudes" for Kingdom employees. Every day you will be offered an opportunity to surrender, or re-commit, some aspect of your life to God. The conditions you'll address represent places where there may be brokenness in your heart as the result of living in the world and suffering the attacks of the Enemy.

Believe it or not, God desires for you to be whole far more than He desires that you accomplish great feats in His name. He will work His amazing transformation in your heart through the ministrations of the Holy Spirit. Then He'll empower you to meet His Kingdom performance expectations. God will do, in and through you, what you cannot do for yourself. No one will be more thrilled with your success than your Employer and Father!

Let's be very clear about something else related to the topic of our performance and God's response to it. God's love is unconditional. It is a free gift that He has given to you through His son Jesus. Nothing can change God's love for you—it will always be perfect, unconditional and steadfast.

His blessing, on the other hand, is conditional. Obedience and surrender are His requirements for those who desire to experience the manifestation of His promises. This is an extremely important concept. If you fail to understand this, you run the risk of trying to earn God's blessing through your works, rather than responding to God's grace with obedience as a sign of your love for Him.

This could lead you into the same deception that kept the Pharisees from realizing who Jesus was and accepting the grace they desperately needed. Here's what Jesus had to say to them: *"Well did Isaiah prophesy of you hypocrites, as it is written: 'This people honors Me with their lips, but their heart is far from Me. And in vain they worship Me, teaching as doctrines the commandments of men'"* (Mark 7:6-7 NKJV). These men had lost sight of love for God and had gotten caught up in empty acts and outward behaviors. Once again you see that Kingdom life is about the condition of the heart.

By the way, none of God's employment expectations are like the "success formulas" that the world is forever marketing. You cannot please God except in a personal relationship with Him. There will never be a time when you will "get it" and be able to run off without Jesus to do your own thing. In your work life, the rule will ever be as Jesus has stated above, *"apart from me you can do nothing"* and...

SPEAK IT OUT:

· I am a laborer for the Lord. God working in me will accomplish His purposes.

· By the empowerment of the Holy Spirit I can do all that I am called to do.

· I thank God that He has made me righteous in Jesus and fit to serve in His Kingdom.

My Journal Notes

DAY BE FREE

> *"Therefore if the Son makes you free,*
> *you shall be free indeed."*

- JOHN 8:36 NKJV

Your Heavenly Father's economy is not affected by unemployment, layoffs or economic bad news of any kind. His ability to provide for you is not limited to any company's payroll department. You have been set free from this world's economy and your future is not dependent on any employer. The apostle Paul puts it this way: *"You have died with Christ, and he has set you free from the spiritual powers of this world. So why do you keep on following the rules of the world?"* (Colossians 2:20 NLT). To buy into all the negative messages about unemployment is to continue to play by the rules of the world that no longer apply to you. You work for God, remember?

Be set free—don't let resentment, bitterness or depression hold you captive. No matter what happens in the workplace, the world cannot keep you from the future God has for you. Live and work in the liberty of the Kingdom of God! As His child and employee you can confidently declare: *"We know that in all things God works for the good of those who love him, who have been called according to his purpose"* (Romans 8:28).

Don't dwell on the wrongs done to you, the unfair treatment you've experienced or the people who failed to recognize your value. Playing those thoughts over and over in your mind is a snare that will anchor you to the past. "The past does not have to be your prison. You have a voice in your destiny. You have a say in your life. You have a choice in the path you take."[17]

---

[17] Max Lucado, *When God Whispers Your Name*, Thomas Nelson, Nashville, TN, 1994, Ch. 15—Overcoming Your Heritage, Kindle edition.

Fill your heart and mind with the new rules of Kingdom employment—forgive those who have mistreated you and release them into God's hands. You just claim your freedom, move on and...

 ## Speak it out:

- · I am free of the systems of this world for I belong to the Kingdom of God.

- · By faith I receive the liberty Christ has given to me. I walk like one who is completely free.

- · I trust in the Word of God and the completed work of Christ Jesus. The world has no hold on me.

 ## Walk it out:

Let It Go! Pick one unhappy memory from your current or previous work experience. Reflect on it...who was involved, what was said, how did you respond, how did you feel? Do you still have the emotional feelings that accompanied this experience? If so, surrender the experience to Jesus.

Imagine yourself in the place of the woman standing completely bent over before the Lord. Tell Jesus that you know He can heal your heart and your mind. Now hear Him respond exactly as he did to her. *"When Jesus saw her, he called her forward and said to her, 'Woman, you are set free from your infirmity'"* (Luke 13:12). Now take a deep breath, let all the hurt and emotion melt away and receive the peace of God. Whenever that memory returns, remind yourself that Jesus has healed it. Repeat this process whenever old hurts and painful memories return. Then go into the workplace unencumbered.

My Journal Notes

DAY 2   BE FRUITFUL

*"Therefore I tell you that the kingdom of God
will be taken away from you and given to a people
who will produce its fruit."*

- MATTHEW 21:43

Your objective is not to gain wealth or a comfortable position for yourself, but to bear fruit for the Kingdom. In Isaiah we learn what fruit God desires: *"Is not this the kind of fasting I have chosen: to loose the chains of injustice and untie the cords of the yoke, to set the oppressed free and break every yoke? Is it not to share your food with the hungry and to provide the poor wanderer with shelter— when you see the naked, to clothe him, and not to turn away from your own flesh and blood?"* (Isaiah 58:6-7). If you examine the life of Jesus, you'll see the fruitful life in action. Everywhere He went and in every action He took He was focused on loving people into the Kingdom of God.

Now take a hard look at the behavior of many who identify themselves as Christians in the workplace. Are they known more for their compassion, mercy, forgiveness and grace or for their judgment and criticism of others? Do they distinguish themselves through their obvious love for other believers or for the speed at which they take offense? If you were to take away the Bibles on their desks and the crosses from around their necks, would there be enough evidence of their identification with the real Jesus Christ to convict them of being His followers?

What about you—would you be found in this unloving, religious group, too? Or, perhaps you are still so aligned with the world's system that others wouldn't know you are a believer at all unless you told them. Neither of these alternatives is the witness to which Christ calls you.

No matter where you work and no matter what work you perform, God expects you to display the love of Christ everywhere and every day. The theme from Isaiah appears again: *"For I was hungry, and you fed me. I was thirsty, and you gave me a drink. I was a stranger, and you invited me into your home. I was naked, and you gave me clothing. I was sick, and you cared for me. I was in prison, and you visited me"* (Matthew 25:35-36 NLT). Given that criteria, are you producing fruit?

If you want to inherit the Kingdom...

 ## Speak it out:

· I am connected to the Vine of abundant life and I bear much fruit.

· I believe in the power of the finished work of Jesus Christ and invite His Spirit to work through me.

· The love of Jesus pours through me into the workplace. I am a laborer in the harvest field.

 ## Walk it out:

Busy Signals: Think about starting a new job. How much attention do you give to discovering your employer's top priorities and expectations? Have you given God that type of attention? Take a few minutes right now and list, in writing, the behaviors most important to God according to Jesus.

How many did you come up with? Did your list include His expectations about your treatment of your enemies? What about the stewardship of your talents and resources? Did you cover everything, or are there some things that you might have missed? Make it your top priority to thoroughly learn your role in God's workforce and make a difference.

My Journal Notes

DAY **BE FORWARD FACING**

"No one who puts a hand to the plow and looks back is fit for service in the kingdom of God."

- LUKE 9:62

Today's verse instructs you to keep your eyes on the future. If you lose your job, or know that a lay-off is coming, don't look back and don't fight to hang on. Jesus says this in today's verse and again in Luke 6:30: *"Give to anyone who asks; and when things are taken away from you, don't try to get them back"* (NLT). Never beg or bargain to keep a job out of fear of the unknown. You are a Child of God, and you are not desperate! Let go and let God take you to a new place where you can learn, grow and contribute again. Maybe you're grieving the loss of a job because you loved the work you were doing. That just proves that you have the capacity to love your work and do it with excellence. Your former position wasn't the only place you could experience such satisfaction. Trust God to put you in another assignment that you can excel in and enjoy.

Perhaps the harder thing to deal with is the realization that there is no security in this world. While that discovery is really painful, it's better to know the truth than to continue to believe that there's a safe and secure job out there somewhere. Let God become your only source of security and you'll never be shaken again. Jesus makes a promise no other employer will ever make: *"I am the gate; whoever enters through me will be saved. He will come in and go out, and find pasture"* (John 10:9). Jesus, your Good Shepherd, will show you a new path into the workplace and a new pasture. A time of employment transition could be the most important, faith-growing time of your life. Put your hand in God's hand to see where He'll lead you and...

Speak it out:

· I know I am not alone and that my security is in God.

· I release the past and look forward to my future in Christ.

· By faith I receive all that I need to move in and out of the workplace without fear.

Walk it out:

In Your Corner: Today it's time to focus on your references. Have you determined who can best tell others about your work performance and character? This is especially important if there is a chance that your former employer will not give you a good reference. Don't treat this important activity casually. Take the time to identify key people—peers, former managers, professional associates and even customers—who will be able to provide a clear picture of your capabilities. Make sure you have accurate and current contact information for these individuals. Then call each one to ask permission to use them as references. Provide them with the current copy of your resume and make sure they understand your job objective. You might even want to ask each one to highlight the specific attributes about you or accomplishments. In this way you can make sure that a prospective employer will get a complete understanding of your skills and abilities.

My Journal Notes

DAY 4 — BE FORTHCOMING

"If anyone is ashamed of me and my words,
the Son of Man will be ashamed of him
when he comes in his glory and in the glory
of the Father and of the holy angels."

- LUKE 9:26

Just in case you haven't already noticed, now that you are a citizen and employee in God's Kingdom, you are a stranger and alien in this world. You aren't supposed to be inconspicuous, so get over it! Your fellow workers ought to recognize you as a Christ follower because:

- You don't use God's name or that of His Son casually or as a curse.

- You don't join in gossip or say hurtful things about others.

- You are silent when others are whining, complaining and bad-mouthing your employer.

- You don't find dirty or mean-spirited jokes funny.

- You give thanks over your food and credit God with every good thing that happens.

- You are calm in the face of bad news and difficult circumstances.

- You offer to pray for people when you hear of their challenges and needs.

- You respond with love, not offense, when others hurt you.

You get the idea. There is no need for you to point out the shortcomings of others—they already know plenty about their failures and inadequacies. Your job is to meet people right where they are and serve them. When others are condemning, bring the compassion of Jesus into the scene. It's amazing how even the greatest of cynics and mockers will show up at your desk to ask for prayers and help when a crisis hits. Make sure your coworkers know you're ready to support and help them whenever they need it. Shine out with the love of Jesus. There's a dark and hurting world that needs the light!

Let this verse from Acts 4:13 be true of you: *"Now when they saw the boldness of Peter and John, and perceived that they were uneducated and untrained men, they marveled. And they realized that they had been with Jesus"* (NLT). If you are ready to be bold because you, too, have been with Jesus…

SPEAK IT OUT:

· Jesus loves me and I have to share His love.

· With the help of the Holy Spirit I am at peace no matter what happens. My trust is in God.

· I bring love and light into the workplace and serve as my Master served.

WALK IT OUT:

Telephone Trust: Today, as you make your phone calls to colleagues, recruiters, network contacts and employers, pay careful attention to your voice and presentation. Are you smiling as you speak? The listener can tell. If you don't convey energy and enthusiasm in your voice, the listener may never become engaged enough in your conversation to hear what you have to say. Another tip: Keep your word. If you ask for two minutes of someone's time, stop the conversation when your time is up. Don't continue the conversation without their permission to do so. Courtesy and attention to detail is perceived as excellence. That's Kingdom behavior. Every time you pick up that phone, sound like someone who has good news to share—because you do! Oh, and if you get the opportunity (or feel the urging of the Holy Spirit), tell someone about the great gift of Jesus Christ!

My Journal Notes

My Journal Notes

BE FORGIVING

"But love your enemies, do good to them,
and lend to them without expecting to get
anything back. Then your reward will be great,
and you will be sons of the Most High."

- LUKE 6:35

Just as there is a zero tolerance policy for fear in the Kingdom, so, too, is there a strict policy about forgiveness. Recall the story Jesus told about the servant who refused to forgive the debt owed to him:

"Then the master called the servant in. 'You wicked servant,' he said, 'I canceled all that debt of yours because you begged me to. Shouldn't you have had mercy on your fellow servant just as I had on you?' In anger his master turned him over to the jailers to be tortured, until he should pay back all he owed. This is how my heavenly Father will treat each of you unless you forgive your brother from your heart" (Matthew 18:32-35).

When Peter asked, *"Lord, how often shall my brother sin against me, and I forgive him? Up to seven times?' Jesus said to him, 'I do not say to you, up to seven times, but up to seventy times seven'"* (Matthew 18:21-22 NKJV).

Jesus is emphatic about forgiveness because He loves you and desires to protect you! Unforgiveness is a "heart disease" that will kill you. It produces bitterness, resentment and anger and it opens you to sin. Gratitude for the mercy you've received, on the other hand, produces love and the desire to extend mercy to others. Never forget how much you need forgiveness, the price Christ paid for it, and how wonderful it feels to be set free by grace. Don't forfeit that for any reason or any person.

Fill yourself with the love of Christ by abiding in Him, and forgiveness will become your nature as it is His. Love you enemies with His love and receive the great reward God promises. If you desire to always forgive and be completely forgiven…

Speak it out:

- I know I have been forgiven much, and I quickly forgive with the same grace I've received.

- By faith I accept God's forgiveness and never mention the confessed sins that God has forgotten.

- I thank God that His mercies are new every morning and that I cannot outlive His grace.

Walk it out:

Make It Good: Sometimes forgiveness also entails making amends. As you think about your work behaviors of the past, are there people to whom you owe a sincere apology? Look beyond coworkers and the workplace. Have family members, friends or members of your church been hurt by your work behaviors or career pursuits? This would be a perfect time to seek forgiveness and restoration insofar as it is up to you to do so. Don't try to control the other person's response. Whether they accept your apology or not is up to them. Your part is to admit to your wrongdoing and seek to make things right. And if that means restitution beyond the apology, follow the model shown by Zacchaeus in Luke 19:1-10 and do it.

My Journal Notes

WEEK 7

KINGDOM GUIDELINES

*"Yet a time is coming and has now come
when the true worshipers will worship the Father
in spirit and truth, for they are the kind
of worshipers the Father seeks. God is spirit, and his
worshipers must worship in the Spirit and in truth."*

- JOHN 4:23-24

You have covered a lot of ground in the past six weeks. You may be finding it difficult to keep everything you've learned in mind as you go through your workday. For this reason you're going to take a week to review five simple guidelines that will reinforce the key principles of Kingdom employment and remind you how important it is that you apply them. This is how you live a life of worship before the Lord.

1. **Put first things first.** You are working for the Kingdom of God. This invisible Kingdom has its foundation in the spiritual realm. To fully trust God, live in obedience to His laws and access His provisions you will have to *live by faith.*

2. **Fear not!** Fear in all its many forms is a device of the Enemy to destroy you and rob you of your Kingdom rights and privileges. More than that it is unbelief and a clear expression of doubt in the goodness of God. You have nothing to fear. Jesus conquered the Enemy, fear and death at Calvary. Now, defended by the perfect love of God, let fear have no hold on you. *Listen to the words of Jesus—"Don't be afraid; just believe"* (Mark 5:36).

3. **Follow the Spirit.** This gift, the indwelling Spirit of God Himself, is the greatest source of power in your life and work. With the Holy Spirit you have access to the mind of Christ and the heart of God. All you must do is accept this teacher, guide, comforter and advocate and allow yourself to be *led by the Spirit.*

4. **Make connections.** You were created for life as a member of the Body of Christ. As only one part of the body you are not completely on your own. The Kingdom of God won't be the perfect Bride awaiting the return of Jesus until all of God's employees come together to accomplish His purposes. Find your place and offer your gifts and talents to show the world you are Christ's disciple by your *love for His body and service to others.*

5. **Stay focused.** Every workday you enter a battlefield in the workplace and join in a fight for the hearts of workers. If you forget where you are standing and what is at stake, you can get hurt. Your safety zone is narrow and obedience to God is the only way you'll achieve your destiny. To ensure you'll succeed, *keep your eyes on Jesus.* And, as always...

SPEAK IT OUT:

· I align my will with the will of God. In Him all my needs are met and desires satisfied.

· I live by faith in God's Kingdom. My foundation is sure and trustworthy.

· Jesus is all that I need. His finished work at Calvary has paid for my victory in this life.

My Journal Notes

_____

_____

_____

_____

_____

_____

_____

_____

_____

_____

_____

_____

_____

My Journal Notes

DAY 1 PUT FIRST THINGS FIRST

"I tell you the truth, if you have faith and do not doubt, not only can you do what was done to the fig tree, but also you can say to this mountain, 'Go, throw yourself into the sea,' and it will be done."

— MATTHEW 21:21

It was by the faith given to you by God that you were saved and born again. Then by an act of that same faith you accepted the righteousness of Jesus as your own. Now it's time for you to live by faith. Remember, at the time of your salvation you were kicked out of the world. The laws that govern the world will no longer work for you. As a citizen of the Kingdom you *"live by faith, not by sight"* (2 Corinthians 5:7). Oh, and you cannot live by both faith and sight because they rarely agree!

Here's how it works: *"This Good News tells us how God makes us right in his sight. This is accomplished from start to finish by faith. As the Scriptures say, "It is through faith that a righteous person has life"* (Romans 1:17 NLT). Another translation puts it this way: "The righteous will live by faith." If you don't learn to live and walk in faith, Kingdom laws won't work for you and you'll be caught on the battlefield, unarmed and defenseless. So here are three key things to know about living by faith:

1. Faith is your title deed for the things God has promised you. *"Now faith is the substance of things hoped for, the evidence of things not seen"* (Hebrews 11:1 NKJV).

2. You must hear God's Word and His promises for them to get down into your heart and transform your thinking. *"Consequently, faith comes from hearing the message, and the message is heard through the word of Christ"* (Romans 10:17).

3. Nothing will persuade your mind and body that you mean business like the faith-filled words that come out of your own mouth. *"'I believed; therefore I have spoken.' With that same spirit of faith we also believe and therefore speak"* (2 Corinthians 4:13).

If you understand that a life of faith is your only option...

Speak it out:

· My mouth is filled with words of faith. I speak what the Holy Spirit tells me to say.

· I choose to live by faith in Jesus and the promises of His Word.

· I know God's Word is true and trustworthy, and I find all my answers there.

Walk it out:

High Level Communications: Do you write out your prayer requests? If not, take a moment and write down the top three requests that you have before the Lord right now. Are you guilty of asking for specific outcomes that may or may not be the will of God? Change your requests from what you want to what God wants for you. Spend your prayer time asking for the bigger gifts—provision, guidance, joy and peace. Trust the Lord to determine the best way to satisfy all your requests.

My Journal Notes

DAY 2   FEAR NOT

"Do not be afraid; only believe."

- MARK 5:36 NKJV

Fear could be described as faith in the Enemy. Whenever you entertain fear, in any form, you are making a decision to ignore your Father's promises and believe "the father of lies" instead. God, therefore, has a zero tolerance policy regarding fear. With the repeated command "Fear not!" He makes it clear that it is simply not allowed in His Kingdom or in His workforce. It's up to you to enforce that policy in your life.

Be assured, if fear was necessary, God would have provided it but He didn't: *"For God has not given us a spirit of fear, but of power and of love and of a sound mind"* (2 Timothy 1:7 NKJV). Fear gains a foothold whenever you question if God still loves you and if He's really looking out for you. So the antidote to fear, when you feel yourself succumbing to it, is more time in God's presence. *"There is no fear in love. But perfect love drives out fear"* (1 John 4:18). Do what Jesus commands in today's verse. Don't fear, just believe in God's love and His promises. Here's your personal formula for success— *"Submit to God. Resist the devil and he will flee from you "* (James 4:7 NJKV).

Unfortunately, fear has a huge foothold in the workplace. Some employers enjoy using it as a tactic to maintain control and manipulate others. In organizations worldwide suggestions for improvement and correction are never brought forward for fear of repercussions and punishment. Lives are lived out of balance for fear of job loss or losing position to someone else. Unfortunately, fear has become such an integral part of society that now many think it's entertaining to be frightened. Fear has become fun. It will take your fixed determination and strong faith to refuse to join into the pervasive climate of fear in today's marketplace.

The spiritual armor described in Ephesians 6:11-12 will help you take your stand if you'll remember to use it. Keep yourself filled with God's truth, empowered by Christ's righteousness, guarded by your faith, and defended by the sword of His Word and Spirit. If you know the battle is real and the stakes are high...

 ## Speak it out:

- I have all that I need to win every battle against the Enemy and in the workplace.

- By faith I am empowered to use all of God's weapons.

- I stand firm because I have been well trained and perfectly equipped.

 ## Walk it out:

Keep the Ball in Your Court: For some reason, job seekers frequently give away their control over the employment process. Don't do that. Don't ask the employer to follow up with you, make the follow up calls yourself. Call repeatedly to secure an interview; don't wait to see if you make it through the screening process. Instead of asking others to call their connections on your behalf, get the names and introduce yourself. Your promise is that you'll receive if you keep asking and keep knocking, so do it.

My Journal Notes

DAY 3   FOLLOW THE SPIRIT

"But when he, the Spirit of truth, comes,
he will guide you into all truth.
He will not speak on his own; he will speak
only what he hears, and he will tell you
what is yet to come."

- JOHN 16:13

"And it shall come to pass in the last days, says God, That I will pour out of My Spirit on all flesh; Your sons and your daughters shall prophesy, Your young men shall see visions, Your old men shall dream dreams. And on My menservants and on My maidservants I will pour out My Spirit in those days; And they shall prophesy" (Joel 2:28 and Acts 2:16-18 NKJV).

When Jesus showed Himself to His disciples after the Resurrection, He said, *"'Peace be with you! As the Father has sent me, I am sending you.' And with that he breathed on them and said, 'Receive the Holy Spirit'"* (John 20:22). With the Holy Spirit, the disciples received the power they would need to fulfill their mission. As John the Baptist had prophesized, Jesus baptized His disciples with the Holy Spirit and fire. The Holy Spirit is so awesome that Jesus declared *"Nevertheless I tell you the truth. It is to your advantage that I go away; for if I do not go away, the Helper will not come to you; but if I depart, I will send Him to you"* (John 16:7 NKJV).

This Helper, the indwelling Holy Spirit, is now yours—to comfort, guide, lead, remind and empower you. Jesus did not begin His ministry until He received the Holy Spirit. You, too, need the Holy Spirit to accomplish what God has assigned you to do. And you need to be led by the Spirit in order to overcome the challenges and avoid the snares of the workplace and the world.

If you don't personally know the third Person of the Trinity, now is the time to get acquainted. Study what the Word of God has to say concerning the Holy Spirit—don't just rely on the opinions of others. The Book of Acts, Chapter 19, is a great place to start. Greet the Spirit and...

SPEAK IT OUT:

· I am the temple of the Holy Spirit of God. He lives in me.

· By faith I receive the full revelation of the Holy Spirit that I might walk in power and authority.

· With the power of the Holy Spirit, I work to advance the Kingdom of God on earth.

WALK IT OUT:

Listen Up! How well do you listen? Do you really pay attention to others? Listening is probably the number one job search skill. It heads the list of relationship building skills and work skills as well. But you'll never learn to listen well until you learn to put others first and forget yourself long enough to hear what they really have to say. Distinguish yourself by becoming the most attentive listener people encounter in their day. Practice really listening to your family, friends and the people you meet so you'll be ready to hear what employers are looking for and respond with excellence. Start by carefully attending to the "still, small voice" of the Spirit within.

My Journal Notes

DAY **MAKE CONNECTIONS**

"My prayer is not for them alone. I pray also for those who will believe in me through their message, that all of them may be one, Father, just as you are in me and I am in you. May they also be in us so that the world may believe that you have sent me. I have given them the glory that you gave me, that they may be one as we are one."

- JOHN 17:20-22

Is church just a place you go on Sundays? Do you actually know the people you sit with each week? *"Pointing to his disciples, he [Jesus] said, 'Here are my mother and my brothers. For whoever does the will of my Father in heaven is my brother and sister and mother'"* (Matthew 12:49-50). As you sit beside them in church each Sunday, do you know if your true family members are unemployed and struggling? Do you know what's going on in their lives? You are an essential part of the Body of Christ and your family needs your involvement. Romans 12:10-13 gives us insight into what God has in mind: *"Be kindly affectionate to one another with brotherly love, in honor giving preference to one another; not lagging in diligence, fervent in spirit, serving the Lord; rejoicing in hope, patient in tribulation, continuing steadfastly in prayer; distributing to the needs of the saints, given to hospitality"* (NKJV).

Unfortunately, many believers also take their education, experience, skills and energy to the workplace first. They market themselves to the world in hopes of fame and fortune, giving only the leftovers of their time and talents to the Church. Some aren't serving in the Body of Christ at all. What about you? How connected are you in the fellowship of believers? Are you working in unity and as one with other believers, demonstrating the power of the good news of Jesus Christ to the world?

The workplace may well be your mission field, but don't forget about your church. With the combined efforts and talents of all its members, the Church can reach the world with Christ's message in a way you cannot, on your own. And in your church, your skills and talents may provide the life support someone really needs, so share and...

SPEAK IT OUT:

- I am an essential part of the Body of Christ and serve in accordance with my design.

- By faith I show that I am Jesus' disciple by my love for my brothers and sisters in Christ.

- I live in unity with all fellow believers and with them demonstrate God's love for all the world.

WALK IT OUT:

Get the Word Out: Who do you know who knows lots of people? We all know someone with many connections to others...a hairdresser, lawyer, insurance salesman, or educator, for example. Have you asked this well-connected person to help you with your employment search? Today make an appointment to speak with this person specifically about the work you want to be doing. When you meet, try to discover who this person might know who could bring you closer to the source of your next work assignment. In this process you're not looking for open positions, you're looking for people who know people. Get the names and contact them. Trust the Lord to open the way before you.

My Journal Notes

DAY 5 STAY FOCUSED

"And you will hear of wars and rumors of wars.
See that you are not troubled; for all these
things must come to pass.... And there will be
famines, pestilences, and earthquakes in various
places....And then many will be offended, will
betray one another, and will hate one another.
Then many false prophets will rise up and deceive
many. And because lawlessness will abound,
the love of many will grow cold. But he who
endures to the end shall be saved."

- MATTHEW 24:6-14 NKJV

Peter took his eyes off Jesus and he began to sink. The same thing is likely to happen to you today in all the chaos of the workplace. The things Jesus describes in today's scripture are the realities of life now. In the face of all that's going on, the divided attention many believers give Jesus is insufficient. You need to keep your focus on Jesus too! *"The eye is the lamp of the body. If your eyes are good, your whole body will be full of light. But if your eyes are bad, your whole body will be full of darkness. If then the light within you is darkness, how great is that darkness!"* (Matthew 2:22-23 NIV) It may seem an insignificant thing to spend time listening to naysayers and immersing yourself in the world's reports. In actuality, entertaining their fears and doubts just might take you out of the running.

You cannot afford to be casual about this. Follow the apostle Paul *"looking unto Jesus, the author and finisher of our faith, who for the joy that was set before Him endured the cross, despising the shame, and has sat down at the right hand of the throne of God"* (Hebrews 12:2 NKJV).

Your focus on Kingdom objectives must be intense as well. In Revelation 3:16, Jesus addresses the matter this way: *"So, because you are lukewarm— neither hot nor cold—I am about to spit you out of my mouth."* For your own sake and that of the Kingdom, you must keep yourself from becoming distracted.

Use every opportunity afforded by your work and your involvement in your church to bring the Gospel to others. Live an authentic and compassionate life in service to others. Never forget that you are God's employee first and foremost. Your work and conduct should be so excellent that you cause others to glorify Him and be drawn to His Kingdom. Stay focused and…

SPEAK IT OUT:

· I am focused on Jesus and my faith is growing.

· By faith I accept my place in Christ at the right hand of God.

· Because I am in Christ, I live a victorious life.

WALK IT OUT:

You Win! When was the last time you spent time reflecting on the awesome gift that Jesus gave to you on the day of your salvation? Take time today to praise Him for His sacrifice. Think about the value that you place on the gift of eternal life and absolute forgiveness. What is that worth in the grand scheme of things? It helps to have an eternal perspective on life and to realize what really matters. As you go through the job search process and deal with day-to-day issues, never forget that life's most awesome reward has already been given to you—the priceless gift of eternal life in Jesus Christ.

My Journal Notes

WEEK

KINGDOM WORK HABITS

"And so I tell you, keep on asking, and you will receive
what you ask for. Keep on seeking, and you will find.
Keep on knocking, and the door will be opened to you."

- LUKE 11:9

This promise is your assurance that you will find His Kingdom, and the perfect satisfaction of every request that aligns with the will of God, if you keep going. But that's the hard part—to keep on when nothing appears to be happening. There's a tendency to think that when things don't happen immediately it means that God is not answering prayer. That's just not true. God always answers prayer, and many times He uses apparent delays and seasons of waiting to build Kingdom work habits in His employees. "Abram went through thirteen years of silence, but in those years all of his self-sufficiency was destroyed. He grew past the point of relying on his own common sense. Those years of silence were a time of discipline, not a period of God's displeasure." [18]

Research indicates that a habit can be formed in as few as ten days, given many repetitions. However, most habits take months to develop. Then the longer a desired behavior is practiced and the more frequently

---

[18] Oswald Chambers, *My Utmost for His Highest, Discovery House Publishers*, Grand Rapids, MI, 1992, Devotional for January 19—"Vision and Darkness."

it is repeated, the stronger that habit will become. So, despite the world's microwave mentality and desire for instant gratification, it's apparent that our character and spiritual maturity must be built over time.

This week you'll review five work habits God expects of His employees. Developing them is some of the really hard work of Kingdom life. You'll need to keep working on these habits with no visible sign of progress or reward for long periods of time. You may even feel like you're working alone as Jesus steps back to let you build your spiritual muscle. Just don't give up. Everyone wins, you and those around you, when you:

- **Give thanks** to God as your automatic response in every circumstance.(Ephesians 5:20)
- **Bear fruit** in the workplace, as Christ's love works through you. (John 15:5)
- **Hang in there** with patience and faithful perseverance. Allow God to complete His work in you and on your behalf. (James 1:4)
- **Practice your serve** demonstrating your commitment to Christ's commands and loving others until He returns. (John 13:14)
- **Find treasure** because you look for it, knowing God's blessing is active in your life. (Matthew 13:44)

 ## SPEAK IT OUT:

· I have faith in the Word of God, and I know that the right doors will always open for me.

· I am determined to seek the Kingdom first and to receive all that God has for me.

· By faith I exercise God's ask, seek and knock strategy of Kingdom life.

My Journal Notes

DAY 1   GIVE THANKS

*"Father, I thank you that you have heard me.
I knew that you always hear me, but I said
this for the benefit of the people standing here,
that they may believe that you sent me."*

- JOHN 11:41-42

Giving thanks continually ought to be the hallmark of every believer! One of the best explanations of, and rationales for, thanksgiving in the New Testament is in 2 Corinthians 9:10-12. *"Now he who supplies seed to the sower and bread for food will also supply and increase your store of seed and will enlarge the harvest of your righteousness. You will be enriched in every way so that you can be generous on every occasion, and through us your generosity will result in thanksgiving to God. This service that you perform is not only supplying the needs of the Lord's people but is also overflowing in many expressions of thanks to God."*

How can you respond with anything other than thanksgiving when God meets, not only your immediate needs, but also promises to provide all you will ever need in your future? Then, He enriches you *in every way…* materially, spiritually, mentally and emotionally according to His perfect grace, so that you will be in a position to be generous to others *on every occasion* (2 Corinthians 9:8-11). If you have ever experienced the joy of being in exactly the right place to meet the needs of someone else, you will appreciate this wonderful promise.

Every time Jesus blessed people by feeding, healing or even raising them from the dead, He acknowledged the Father whose power made it possible. When you consider all that the Father has already done for you through the saving work of Jesus Christ, and all that He will continue to do in your life, it's easy to feel grateful, isn't it? Don't you wish there were a better and bigger way to show your gratitude than simply saying "Thank you?" If you agree...

Speak it out:

· I thank God publicly, for I know He always meets all my needs.

· I have confidence in the Word and receive boldness to give thanks to Him before others.

· I accept my assignment to strengthen others with my prayers and attitude of gratefulness.

Walk it out:

Gratitude Log: Most job seekers could use a little encouragement from time to time. So today, call someone who worked closely with you in the past and ask them to share what they observed about your strengths, gifts and talents. Let that person tell you what you're good at and how you contributed to the workplace.

Write down what they say. Ask the Holy Spirit to help you prepare CAR stories based on their input. These are examples of your work successes detailed in the <u>C</u>ONDITIONS you faced, the <u>A</u>CTIONS you took and the <u>R</u>ESULTS you achieved. (See *Employed for Life*, pp. 137-138.) You can then share these CAR stories at your next performance review or with prospective employers.

Next, create a gratitude log. Thank God for your skills and abilities and for the opportunities you've had to use them in the work place. To keep the journal going, write down five things you're grateful for each night. See how many days you can go before repeating yourself.

My Journal Notes

DAY 2 — BEAR FRUIT

"I am the true vine, and my Father is the gardener. He cuts off every branch in me that bears no fruit, while every branch that does bear fruit he prunes so that it will be even more fruitful.

- JOHN 15:1-2

This is one of those scriptures you probably wish Jesus hadn't said! Yet it's essential to know that God will prune you, even in your most fruitful endeavors and areas of greatest service, and that you will undergo periods of dormancy that are by God's design and for your good. You need to know that your Employer is going to close down every spiritually unprofitable aspect of your life—and that's a good thing. It will be a reflection of your spiritual maturity when you stand in faith as He prunes you.

In referring to Himself and His death, Jesus said, *"I tell you the truth, unless a kernel of wheat falls to the ground and dies, it remains only a single seed. But if it dies, it produces many seeds"* (John 12:24). This principle also applies to you as His follower. The small seeds you plant for the fruit of the Spirit in your life may be invisible to others. You may even be criticized for your failure to be like Jesus. Your dreams of Kingdom successes may also disappear from sight and you'll wonder if they've died. In these times of darkness you will have to simply trust God and keep doing what He has commanded. Don't blame the Enemy, although I'm sure he delights in your dark moments, or wonder if God has abandoned you; just trust and wait in faith. The harvest will come in God's perfect timing.

Seasons of silence and waiting may be the hardest to bear, but this is when your roots will grow deeper and become stronger. Just stay close to

Jesus as you wait. He is the vine and you are a branch. If you know that when you abide in Him, no matter what comes, you will bear good fruit...

 ## SPEAK IT OUT:

· I am focused on Jesus and my faith is growing.

· By faith I accept my place in Christ at the right hand of God.

· Because I am in Christ, I live a victorious life.

 ## WALK IT OUT:

Examine the Produce: Take a moment and reflect on your time in the workplace. As you consider what you've accomplished, do you think about the lives you've changed for the better? Remember, God is interested in influence and relationships. He has called you to be a healing, encouraging, life-giving force in the lives of others. It's easy to get caught up in the work that needs to be done and ride roughshod over those who appear to get in the way. Far too many workers focus only on the tasks at hand and not the people they work with to accomplish those tasks. Using God's priorities for love and relationships, have you been in the business of producing good fruit or bad? In the latter case, repent and within reason seek forgiveness from those you may have harmed in your zeal.

My Journal Notes

DAY 3 — HANG IN THERE

"Keep on asking, and you will receive what you ask for. Keep on seeking, and you will find. Keep on knocking, and the door will be opened to you. For everyone who asks, receives. Everyone who seeks, finds. And to everyone who knocks, the door will be opened."

- MATTHEW 7:7-8 NLT

When you're sick you have no problem going to a doctor to get a prescription for a drug that promises to help you recover. You are willing to take the medication three times a day for weeks or months if that's what the doctor prescribes aren't you? After one or two pills, if the symptoms persist, you don't stop taking the medication. You just follow the directions on the bottle, believing relief and healing will come. It makes you wonder why believers have such a hard time doing the same thing with the promises of God. Jesus never said that fruit would be produced overnight or discipleship would be easy, did He?

Part of our difficulty in waiting on the Lord just might be found in the world's perspective on the importance of *feelings*. The constant messages to *trust your feelings, go with your feelings*, and do whatever you *feel* like doing are all guaranteed to lead you away from a life rooted in faith alone. Emotions are fickle and cannot be trusted for guidance—ever. When your feelings conflict with God's word and direction, stand your ground and refuse to be moved.

Faithful perseverance has always been God's pattern. Multiple trips around Jericho brought the walls down, multiple dips in the river cleansed Naaman of leprosy. Some miracles take time. Take a stand, set your face like a flint and let patience produce a perfect work in you. Just out of your line of vision, God is orchestrating things on your behalf. Sometimes God waits for others to come into obedience, for the right people to get into position, or for the right factors to be in place in order to work the miracle you need. Sometimes He's stretching you to build your faith. You may have no idea what God is doing behind the scenes but you can rest assured it's for your greatest good because the Word says so. *"And let us not grow weary while doing good, for in due season we shall reap, if we do not faint"* (Galatians 6:9 NKJV). If you believe it...

SPEAK IT OUT:

· I know God's Word is true and His promises are real.

· I am single-minded in my determination to receive the promises of God by faith.

· My eyes are ever open, and I expect to see God's response to every prayer that lines up with His will.

WALK IT OUT:

Kicking and Screaming: How do you measure up in the patience and perseverance category? Take a look at your job search activity. How many calls can you make before deciding to stop for the day? And how many times are you willing to call back in order to get in touch with a key networking contact or prospective employer? How many behavioral examples have you prepared for your interviews? If you're honest with yourself you may discover that you too have fallen victim to today's impatient, microwave-style expectations and behavior. Now is the time to correct that. Decide right now to be consistent and faithful with the help of the Holy Spirit. Work on every available lead, persist until you've made a contact with every targeted employer and prepare for every common interview question. Do your part and trust God to do His.

My Journal Notes

DAY 4   PRACTICE YOUR SERVE

"It will be good for those servants whose master
finds them watching when he comes.
I tell you the truth, he will dress himself to serve,
will have them recline at the table
and will come and wait on them."

- Luke 12:37

The first instruction Jesus gives in Luke 12:35 is: *"Be dressed ready for service and keep your lamps burning."* This is the type of command that you would expect from the Master. Other parables express the same theme—consistency and faithfulness in service is what your Master expects of you.

But today's scripture is truly extraordinary. It's a promise that when the master finds his servants doing what they were instructed to do, he will be so pleased that he will invite them to sit down and will serve them himself! This captures the type of Master we serve. Because of His wonderful grace, He is ready to bless, love, and care for us every chance He gets! Yes, God wants us to love and serve others, ever mindful that He is going to return. He wants to find us completing our assignments when He comes back. The part that is so often overlooked is that *"it will be good"* for you when He returns and you are found laboring in His service.

Paul says it this way: *"Serve wholeheartedly, as if you were serving the Lord, not men, because you know that the Lord will reward everyone for whatever good he does, whether he is slave or free"* (Ephesians 6:7). Like it or not, it's an error to believe that God expects nothing more of us but to confess Jesus as Lord. Lip service alone is not what He's looking for. God expects us to demonstrate our love for Jesus by keeping His commandments just as Jesus kept the commandments of the Father. And Jesus is very clear that it will not go well for any of God's servants if they are being disobedient when He returns (Luke 12:45-46).

If you're unclear about Christ's commandments and what constitutes the faithful service He is looking for, Paul sums it up this way: *"The only thing that counts is faith expressing itself through love"* (Galatians 5:6) and *"he who loves his fellowman has fulfilled the law"* (Romans 13:8). This will be evidenced in your love, without prejudice or partiality (James 2:1-9) and in your devotion to others (Philippians 2:3). No matter how difficult it may be to love as Christ has loved you, if you are committed to His service...

 SPEAK IT OUT:

· By faith I forgive everyone who has hurt me or caused me harm.

· I pray God's blessing and love over all those in my workplace including my employer.

· I have the Holy Spirit in me and I love with the love of Christ, in service to Him.

 WALK IT OUT:

What kind of employee are (were) you? Have you always given your employers your very best every day, as if you were working for Jesus Himself? Are your words and your actions uplifting, encouraging and productive? Why don't you come before the Lord right now, humble and honest, and confess your shortcomings, sins and failures? Don't worry if you feel a strong urge to make excuses, blame others or let yourself off the hook by comparing your performance to others—those are merely simply symptoms of the *heart disease* that Jesus is now healing. Note the behaviors you don't want to carry into your next workplace and ask for help in eliminating them from your life.

My Journal Notes

DAY 5 FIND TREASURE

*"The kingdom of heaven is like treasure
hidden in a field. When a man found it,
he hid it again, and then in his joy went and
sold all he had and bought that field.
Again, the kingdom of heaven is like a merchant
looking for fine pearls. When he found one of
great value, he went away and sold everything
he had and bought it."*

– MATTHEW 13:44-46

Believers ought to be the first to recognize God's blessings when they occur. While others may wonder at the coincidences that you experience, you need to know that God has gone before you and hidden treasures just for you because of His great love for you (Isaiah 45:3). One of the most important Kingdom behaviors to cultivate, right along with gratitude, is the ability to find and recognize God's blessings in your life.

Have you heard the still quiet voice that speaks a personal word of guidance or direction as you seek answers? That is one of the most precious treasures you will ever receive. Do you recognize God's favor at work when you alone are able to get through to a decision maker; when your resume out of hundreds of others captures attention and gets you an interview; and when you receive an offer just before a hiring freeze goes into effect? Favor is a treasure that is often unnoticed or taken for granted. Pay careful attention so that you don't miss God's answers to prayer that just don't look like what you were expecting. He's full of surprises and His ways are most definitely not our ways!

When you comprehend the awesome love God has for you and recognize how He cares for you, you will not be able to suppress the joy that fills your life. *"I have told you these things so that you will be filled with my joy. Yes, your joy will overflow!"* (John 15:11 NLT). If you are beginning to experience this joy...

 ## SPEAK IT OUT:

- I experience the joy of the Lord. My happiness is not based on my circumstances.

- By faith I release any belief that says I should be worried, concerned or sad as I go through my job search. The Spirit leads me forth in joy.

- I receive the Word of God, the things Jesus has told me, and I have joy unspeakable!

 ## WALK IT OUT:

Joy Unspeakable! God offers the extraordinary employment benefit of joy in Christ Jesus. In fact, He wants us so joy filled that it pours out of us and splashes on everyone around us. The joy Jesus felt, that complete joy of God's overwhelming and perfect love for Him, can be yours! Right now, ask Jesus to pour out His joy in your life. There's no reason you can't be completely joyous during your job search. The world can't do this, but believers can, by God's grace.

My Journal Notes

WEEK

KINGDOM WITNESSING

"All authority in heaven and on earth has been given to me. Therefore go and make disciples of all nations, baptizing them in the name of the Father and of the Son and of the Holy Spirit, and teaching them to obey everything I have commanded you. And surely I am with you always, to the very end of the age."

- MATTHEW 28:18-20

You are called to be an ambassador for Jesus Christ (2 Corinthians 5:20). Everywhere you go you are fighting against the Enemy and the world in order to point others toward Christ. Jesus is ready to back you up in the completion of your assignments and destiny.

Given that adults spend most of their waking hours in the workplace, it stands to reason that your most powerful witness will be on the job. Someone once said, "Your life is the only Bible some people will ever read." Your conduct in the workplace is likely to be more compelling to those who have rejected Christianity than any sermon or evangelistic outreach. To make a life-changing difference in the lives of those you work with, the Spirit of the living God is at work in you. You are more than well equipped to reach the world of work for Jesus.

As you discovered at the start of this employment orientation process eight weeks ago, two kingdoms are competing for your heart and your loyalty. You cannot serve both. This week you'll explore some common work opportunities, highlighted below, and make your choice to take a stand for Jesus in your behavior or to continue in the ways of this world.

- Will you buy into the world's idea that only a select few have leadership ability, or will you lead, as a servant of others, in every position you hold?

- Will you strive for authority over others in order to assert your will, or will you use your God-given opportunities to bless the workplace?

- Will your ambition be to create success and worldly gain for yourself, or will you use your passion for the Kingdom, leaving a worthy legacy behind you?

- Will you join the competition for the best of everything in this world, or will you run the race for the prize of a crown to place at Jesus' feet?

- Will you join those searching for security in the world, or will you place all your confidence in your Savior and King?

The following scripture applies to you *"The harvest is plentiful, but the workers are few. Ask the Lord of the harvest, therefore, to send out workers into his harvest field"* (Luke 10:2). Ask to be one of those laborers. Join those in the mission field and in ministry by giving your financial and material resources to support their work. In that way, you can help the Kingdom by bringing the Gospel into the world, sharing in the rewards of God's laborers (Matthew 10:41). But most importantly, be Christ's witness in the place where you work and in your community. If you desire to participate in the harvest of souls as a living example of Kingdom life...

SPEAK IT OUT:

· I choose to be of good cheer and at peace because I am in Christ.

· By faith I receive His overcoming power in the face of every challenge and trial.

· I labor joyfully in the Kingdom for the harvest of souls for Christ.

My Journal Notes

My Journal Notes

DAY 1   LEADERSHIP

"You know that the rulers in this world lord it over their people, and officials flaunt their authority over those under them. But among you it will be different. Whoever wants to be a leader among you must be your servant, and whoever wants to be first among you must become your slave. For even the Son of Man came not to be served but to serve others and to give his life as a ransom for many."

— MATTHEW 20:25-28 NLT

Business owners and leaders in the workplace are always interested in identifying leadership talent. Much energy is spent trying to recognize, hire and retain these "high potential" employees and to groom them for future positions in leadership roles. God is doing the same thing with you, to prepare you as a king and priest to one day reign with Him on earth in His Kingdom which has no end (Revelation 5:10). He designed you for this purpose, chose you out of the world's kingdom, and put you to work in His family business. This life experience is your training ground, and in serving others, you become qualified for your eternal leadership assignment.

The amazing thing is that often those who serve with excellence and passion, as unto the Lord, find themselves placed in leadership positions in the workplace through no effort of their own. Remember, God is intent on drawing all men to Himself, and He will use your relationships and influence to accomplish that purpose. So who, in your work environment, needs your service? Where can you support a fellow worker who is struggling? How can you help your boss be more successful? Commit your skills and talents to God and put yourself to work, serving in your church and on your job, and...

Speak it out:

- Lord, make me in Your image and likeness. I surrender my ego and will to become like You.

- By faith I accept the command to serve others, and with the empowerment of the Holy Spirit I demonstrate the love of Christ.

- I desire to please You alone, Lord, and to prepare for my eternal assignment as a king and priest in God's Kingdom.

Walk it out:

Employer POV (Point of View): As you contact prospective employers today, think about how you can serve their needs. Forget your agenda and focus on theirs. If you're employed, put your boss's needs in the forefront today. How can you make your supervisor more successful? What can you do to improve the quality of your manager's work-life? Take time to listen for the problems they want to solve, the work they need to get done and the type of person they need. If you fit the bill, offer your service. If not, say so and offer to help them find the person they need. Always try to serve other job seekers by passing along job leads, encouragement and suggestions. To repeat a phrase we've already talked about, practice your serve!

My Journal Notes

DAY 2 — AUTHORITY

"I have given you authority to trample on snakes and scorpions and to overcome all the power of the enemy; nothing will harm you."

- LUKE 10:19

The apostle Paul says that you are to *"put on the whole armor of God, that you may be able to stand against the wiles of the devil. For we do not wrestle against flesh and blood, but against principalities, against powers, against the rulers of the darkness of this age, against spiritual hosts of wickedness in the heavenly places"* (Ephesians 6:11-12 NKJV). Jesus spent a good bit of time teaching His disciples about the Enemy and the authority they had in Him, yet today, many believers seem to have forgotten all about these instructions. Let today's scripture remind you again about the authority you've been given in Christ and how you are to use it. Be very clear, this authority belongs to Jesus, not you. At His command you are able to resist the Enemy and send him packing (James 4:7). If you try this on your own you are very likely to end up like the sons of Sceva who took on an evil spirit without the authority of Jesus and came out very badly! (Acts 19:14-16)

It's also time for you stop viewing people in the workplace as your problem and understand that they, too, are struggling against a fallen world. You have the spiritual weapons to deal with the real root of the problem, now use them! Pray for your enemies and those that *"despitefully use you"*—that they might be set free (Matthew 5:44). Ask the Lord to place His hand over your workplace. Pray for your leaders. In the name of Jesus, take a stand against evil practices, prejudice, and apathy and do as God directs you. Don't act on your own, just follow the commands you're given.

Wield your spiritual weapons from a place of submission and service to your employer. Daniel and Joseph modeled this and God blessed their faithfulness to the great benefit of their employers. You can have the same impact wherever you work. Trust the Holy Spirit to guide you and...

SPEAK IT OUT:

- There is no fear in me. Neither man nor devil can defeat me because Jesus has conquered sin and death.

- By faith I act in the authority granted by Jesus to accomplish the purpose to which God has called me.

- The love of Christ works through me for all people. My only adversary is the devil.

WALK IT OUT:

Disobedience by Default. What was the last thing God told you to do that you still haven't acted upon? Here's what Jesus says about the matter: *"But what do you think? A man had two sons, and he came to the first and said, 'Son, go, work today in my vineyard.' He answered and said, 'I will not,' but afterward he regretted it and went. Then he came to the second and said likewise. And he answered and said, 'I go, sir,' but he did not go. Which of the two did the will of his father?"* (Matthew 21:28-31 NKJV). Lip service and good intentions don't equate to obedience, do they? Procrastination is disobedience too. If you are dawdling over doing something God has directed, confess your disobedience, tell God you desire to do what He tells you and then do it.

My Journal Notes

DAY 3   **AMBITION**

*"Do not store up for yourselves treasures on
earth, where moth and rust destroy, and
where thieves break in and steal. But store up for
yourselves treasures in heaven, where moth and
rust do not destroy, and where thieves do not
break in and steal. For where your treasure is,
there your heart will be also."*

- MATTHEW 6:19

Do you know anyone who determined to become a millionaire by a set age? Have you established financial or career goals upon which you are currently focused? What price are you willing to pay in energy and effort to achieve those goals? The most important questions of all are who are you trying to serve with your ambition and is God's will the underlying motivation? If you're going to give an endeavor your best effort and energy, it needs to be a worthy cause, doesn't it? And much as you might want to serve God, it's hard to let go of the idea that success is measured by status and wealth. That's why you need to constantly examine what you're working on and make sure you're aiming at the right target.

By the way, ambition for the right cause is not a problem. Passion and ambition are attributes given by God to fuel the fire for His Kingdom that Jesus started (Luke 12:49). Now He expects you to use your ambition to keep it going! What is it, in the workplace and the world, that really bothers you? What human plight causes you to burn with the righteous anger Jesus directed at the moneychangers in the temple? I'm not talking about self-righteous anger. You must always act with a humble spirit, then get connected to others working to right the same wrong. With the power of God behind you, put your ambition to work to make a difference and...

SPEAK IT OUT:

- With the help of the Holy Spirit I will one day have crowns to place at Jesus' feet.

- Father, I thank You that You will guide me to make an eternal difference for Your Kingdom.

- Let my desires be Your desires, Lord. Give me Your heart for others and show me how to light the way for their salvation.

WALK IT OUT:

Legacy Minded: Today shift your focus from what you hope to build as your career path to the legacy you would like to leave behind, in the workplace, in your family and in your community. Write down the way you would like to be remembered by those around you. Now evaluate where you spent your energy and efforts over the past week or two. Have you taken any actions on a consistent basis that ensure you will leave that legacy? If you hope to be remembered as a great parent but spend no time listening to your children, your chances of achieving that objective aren't good, are they? Write down three practical things you can do in every area of your life to make your desired legacy a reality.

My Journal Notes

DAY 4   COMPETITION

"So the last will be first, and the first last.
For many are called, but few chosen."

- MATTHEW 20:16 NKJV

Look at today's verse and this scripture describing the same Kingdom behavior:

"But when you are invited, take the lowest place, so that when your host comes, he will say to you, 'Friend, move up to a better place.' Then you will be honored in the presence of your fellow guests. For everyone who exalts himself will be humbled, and he who humbles himself will be exalted" (Luke 14:10-11).

Most believers really find these commands difficult to obey; they are so out of step with the world. What it really comes down to is a matter of trust. Do you trust that God is watching out for you or do you still think you have to take care of yourself? Do you trust that God is all powerful, or do you think the organization you work for so big, or your boss so evil, that God is simply not able to help in your present circumstances? If you're still relying on the dog-eat-dog behavior of the world, it could even be that you think God is the problem. Maybe you believe that He hasn't noticed you being overlooked, so you have to get what you want for yourself.

The heart of the matter is this—you either trust that God is sovereign, His will for you is perfect, and His Word is true, or you don't. You either believe that He will work all things together for your good because you love Him and are called according to His purpose (Romans 8:28) or you don't. No matter how you look at it, trusting God to manage competitive workplace situations requires absolute trust in His love for you. You will never know what God will do, until you give Him the opportunity. If you are willing to follow in the Master's footsteps, and accept the lowliest position to wash the feet of others...

SPEAK IT OUT:

· I desire to become like Christ. I work to serve and not to be served.

· The world cannot tell me if I am winning. God alone is my judge.

· By faith I yield my ego and pride to the Lord that I might walk in true humility like Him.

WALK IT OUT:

Kingdom Sportsmanship: Competition is an integral part of our workplace today. The problem is that too many believers are competing for worldly prizes that have no eternal value. What are you aiming for in your career? Ensure that you are exercising discipline, effort and self-control toward a worthy objective. *"Do you not know that in a race all the runners run, but only one gets the prize? Run in such a way as to get the prize. Everyone who competes in the games goes into strict training. They do it to get a crown that will not last, but we do it to get a crown that will last forever"* (1 Corinthians 9:24-25).

My Journal Notes

DAY 5 — JOB SECURITY

"I am the gate; whoever enters through me will be saved. He will come in and go out, and find pasture."

- JOHN 10:9

There is no job security in the world. You won't find any organization that can guarantee cradle-to-grave employment today. Most workers who pursue professions solely to capitalize on predicted growth opportunities and financial stability are still likely to face interruptions in their work and income at some point in their careers. Sadly, these workers frequently end up dissatisfied, stuck in jobs that don't suit their talents or skills as a result of their pursuit of "safe employment." Of course, it's important to pay attention to market trends and to offer your services where and how they are currently needed; you just can't bank on the workplace as your source of provision or security.

That's why today's scripture is such great news in the current marketplace. Jesus is your gate and the workplace is your pasture. No matter what happens, Jesus, is right with you. He will never leave or forsake you. When you move (or are moved) out of one workplace, you will find Him standing at the entrance to another one, ushering you into new pastures with new opportunities for service.

Sadly, many believers never find this source of direction and security. How about you? Do you recognize God's voice when He speaks to you? Can you go to sleep at night confident that you were always in the right place doing the right things all day? If not, ask Him to teach you to listen for His voice, follow His lead and...

Speak it out:

· Jesus is the source of my provision and security; my job or salary is not.

· I thank God that I am never alone or without direction.

· I know that God is good and His plans for me are good and only good.

Walk it out:

Searching for Security: Take a look at your job search objective again. Does it mention the word security anywhere? Is stability something you are asking an employer to provide? Is "guaranteed security" a criterion you consider before pursuing an open position or job lead? Guess what? You won't find it, not in the world. Certainly, you are secure in your position as God's Employee in His Kingdom, but that may not be a "stable" position in the world's vernacular. Given your Employer, you likely will not be allowed to stay and get comfortable anywhere. To work for the Lord means to be ready at any time to go anywhere and do anything that He directs. Look at what Jesus did with the disciples, interrupting their careers and calling them to drop everything to follow Him. They didn't stay in one place and get comfortable; chances are you won't either. That's why it's so important to build your resilience and learn to embrace change. Just keep your confidence in the leading of the Holy Spirit, and you'll find your security in the hands of God.

"The settled happiness and security which we all desire, God withholds from us by the very nature of the world: but joy, pleasure and merriment He has scattered broadcast...The security we crave would teach us to rest our hearts in this world...Our Father refreshes us on the journey with some pleasant inns but will not encourage us to mistake them for home."[19]

[19] C.S. Lewis, *The Quotable Lewis*, Tyndale House Publishers, Wheaton, IL, 1990, pp. 307-308.

My Journal Notes

WEEK

KINGDOM PERSPECTIVES

"For John came neither eating nor drinking, and they say, 'He has a demon.' The Son of Man came eating and drinking, and they say, 'Here is a glutton and a drunkard, a friend of tax collectors and "sinners."' But wisdom is proved right by her actions."

- MATTHEW 11:18-20

All mankind will witness the "proving right" of the Word and wisdom of God at the triumphant return of the Lord. Jesus makes the point time and time again that believers and nonbelievers will be judged by their hearts and the resulting fruitfulness of their lives. *"Make a tree good and its fruit will be good, or make a tree bad and its fruit will be bad, for a tree is recognized by its fruit.... The good man brings good things out of the good stored up in him, and the evil man brings evil things out of the evil stored up in him"* (Matthew 12:33, 35).

This week it will become even clearer to you that the Kingdom of God is nothing like the kingdom of the world. Look at the statements below from the perspective of God's Word and decide if they are true or false.

- Power is the ability to cause others to do what you want them to do.

- Wealth is the means to a happy and comfortable life.

- Purpose is found in exciting work and a profession you love.

- Stewardship requires you to take care of the possessions of someone else. Ownership is better.

- Promotion is the outward indication of the greatness of your talent, ability, cleverness and influence.

While the world strives to get to the top, to be at the front, your Master says: *"Not so with you. Instead, whoever wants to become great among you must be your servant, and whoever wants to be first must be your slave—just as the Son of Man did not come to be served, but to serve, and to give his life as a ransom for many"* (Matthew 20:26-28).

You will need to have Christ's mind on all these concepts in order to work effectively and produce lasting fruit for His Kingdom. Don't be concerned that others will misunderstand why you behave as you do. Over time they will see the fruit of the Spirit manifesting in your life. Indeed, wisdom will be proved right by her deeds. "It is not so much of our time and so much of our attention that God demands; it is not even all our time and all our attention: it is ourselves. For each of us the Baptist's words are true: 'He must increase and I decrease…Let us make up our minds to it; there will be nothing 'of our own' left over to live on; no 'ordinary' life."[20] If you want your life to be extraordinary…

---

[20] C.S. Lewis, *The Weight of Glory and Other Addresses*, Macmillan, New York, NY, 1980, p. 130.

SPEAK IT OUT:

· I am not moved by what I see or feel. I am moved only by the Word of God.

· By faith I demonstrate an eternal perspective in today's chaotic workplace. I am salt and light.

· My loyalty is not divided; I serve God, not the world.

My Journal Notes

My Journal Notes

DAY 1   POWER

"And now I will send the Holy Spirit, just as my Father promised. But stay here in the city until the Holy Spirit comes and fills you with power from heaven."

- LUKE 24:49 NLT

The power the world offers is a counterfeit. In every organization, workers struggle against each other in futile attempts to increase their personal influence and power so they will be in control. What they gain, through the accumulation of money, fame or connections, is nothing more than a temporary and fleeting illusion. Dominion over others is not real power despite what the Enemy would like you to believe.

Real power is simply the ability to get results. Domination of people has nothing to do with it. God, the only source of true power, grants power through the Person of the Holy Spirit to accomplish His purposes. As you might expect, there are no limits to His mighty power. No matter how impossible the task God assigns to you, His power will always provide the strength, tools and opportunity to accomplish it.

Your power—the ability to get results—is found in faith, hope and love. And there is a very important condition attached to it. "No matter what changes God has performed in you, never rely on them. Build only on a Person, the Lord Jesus Christ, and on the Spirit He gives. All our promises and resolutions end in denial because we have no power to accomplish them. When we come to the end of ourselves, not just mentally but completely, we are able to "receive the Holy Spirit."[21]

By the way—if you don't need supernatural power to accomplish what you're trying to do for the Kingdom, you probably aren't exercising your faith

---

[21] Oswald Chambers, *My Utmost for His Highest*, Discovery House Publishers, Grand Rapids, MI, 1992, Devotional January 5.

and obedience in the assignment God has for you. Loving unconditionally and continually forgiving others will take the empowerment of the Spirit. Even the simplest types of work may call for a risk to be taken that will require the power of the Lord to help you to act on it. In fact, you might even need supernatural empowerment just to stay faithful to the assignment you've been given. Kingdom work always requires a partnership with the Holy Spirit in order to get it done. Today as you go through your workday, or employment search, go in the power of the Holy Spirit, which is the love of God. Share it with everyone you meet and...

SPEAK IT OUT:

· I am not afraid even if I should suffer for what is right, I am blessed. (1 Peter 3:13)

· By faith I seek and serve His will.

· Because I am in Christ and He is in me, I work to fulfill the Great Commission. (Matthew 28:18-20)

WALK IT OUT:

Loving Like Jesus: Did you tap into God's power this week? Did you bring compassion, service, peace and encouragement wherever you went? If you still felt the urge to bend someone to your will and assert the right to have your way, you probably weren't walking in the empowerment of the Holy Spirit. As a result you were very likely frustrated and stressed. If you found yourself talking about *yourself, your* circumstances, and *your* needs, it's time to change your focus. Find an opportunity today to do something loving and completely unselfish for someone who needs it. Love like a person who has been filled with the overwhelming love of Jesus Christ.

My Journal Notes

DAY WEALTH

"You say, 'I am rich; I have acquired wealth and do not need a thing.' But you do not realize that you are wretched, pitiful, poor, blind and naked."

- REVELATION 3:17

Where are you placing your trust for your future? If your confidence lies in the growth of your portfolio or bank account or you find yourself trusting a government for your security, you are still participating in the world systems. There is nothing wrong with saving and preparing for the future—good stewards do that. The issue is trust. *"Command those who are rich in this present age not to be haughty, nor to trust in uncertain riches but in the living God, who gives us richly all things to enjoy"* (1 Timothy 6:17 NKJV). As for investing in the future…you're going to spend far more time in eternity than time spent on earth. What is your eternal investment strategy? What are you doing now to obey the command *"store up for yourselves treasures in heaven"?* (Matthew 6:20) Do you even know what you can do today to create that heavenly storehouse?

Allow God to take off your blinders and reveal your beliefs and heart about material and eternal wealth. Ask Him if there is anything you are unwilling to give up at His command? Has any material thing moved from a "possession" to the "possessor"—house, car, comfort, status, youth—anything? Are you placing your confidence in any worldly "safety net" in the place of your true Provider?

Our progress and prosperity, just as that of the rich young ruler in Mark 10:21-22, can be held back when we hang on to things that God tells us to release. If you are stuck in your current employment circumstance, it could be that God is telling you to give up something in order to receive what He has for you. Let go of that hobby or habit that is harming your relationships. Stop playing it safe by staying in an employment situation after its season has ended. Following after the plans of God will always involve an element of risk. That shouldn't come as a surprise—what investment strategy is risk free? It's time to stop placing your hope in a dwindling bank account or some person or government program to rescue you from unemployment. If you are placing your hope in the guidance of the Holy Spirit and trusting God for your provision and future...

SPEAK IT OUT:

· God loves me personally and I know it. My heart is filled with His presence.

· I willingly release anything You require, Lord, knowing You have something far better in mind.

· By faith I obediently accept Your blessing, Lord, and I am made rich without sorrow.

WALK IT OUT:

Salary Expectations: "What are you worth?" That's a silly question because your worth is beyond price. Jesus Christ died for you because He considers you priceless. The world is in no position to overrule the value the Creator has placed on you. Remember that when the salary question comes up in an interview or a performance discussion. The employer is discussing the position's value to the organization and your capability to perform the requirements of that position, not your personal worth. Use a market study or online salary tool to find out the value of the position you're considering.

But, when considering what you're worth, remember the immeasurable value assigned to you by Christ's sacrifice at Calvary.

My Journal Notes

DAY **PURPOSE**

> *"Let your light so shine before men,*
> *that they may see your good works and glorify*
> *your Father in heaven."*
>
> - MATTHEW 5:16 NKJV

Purpose is a concept that many believers truly don't understand. Like citizens of the world they think their purpose has something to do with vocation or profession. Those who have never felt passionate about a work assignment or satisfied with a job often continue to search for purpose.

Today's scripture defines the purpose of every believer's life and it has nothing to do with the occupation or type of work performed. Your purpose in the workplace is for people to see the way you work and the powerful effect that Jesus Christ has had in your life and realize that it is God behind it all. You are here to bring God glory. Your overcoming lifestyle and peace should bring attention to the Kingdom and attract others to it. It's important for you to identify your God-given skills and talents because it is in using them that you will do your best work. The workplace is nothing more than your harvest field and your profession is simply your point of entry.

You work for God. He created you, redeemed you, transformed you, and now showers you with His blessing. He provides strategies that turn seasons of unemployment into seasons of blessing. He makes every kind of workplace challenge into an employment triumph. God stations angels around you to help you and keep you safe (Psalm 91:11).

Your purpose is simply to bring God glory because He alone deserves it. Who besides God cares for you so perfectly and completely? The more you know this God and His love, the more you will shine from the inside out, and the world won't be able to miss it. Take that with you into the workplace and your purpose will be fulfilled. To bring God the glory that He alone deserves…

SPEAK IT OUT:

· I walk in the love and light of God. Christ's love fills me.

· The good works I do are by the grace of God and I give Him all the glory.

· My life is a testimony to the God I serve.

WALK IT OUT:

Short- and Long-Term Goals: It's understood that you are more likely to accomplish your goals if you write them down. Also, make sure they meet S.M.A.R.T criteria. Make sure each goal is Specific (in terms of behavior desired), Measurable, Actionable (there are actions you can take to move forward), Realistic (your planned actions are possible), and Time-bound (you've set a deadline for yourself). With employment goals, just as with the achievement of your legacy, the journey of a thousand miles starts with a single step. So write down your goals and get moving. Don't forget to set goals to accomplish the five workplace blessings in addition to your employment objectives: a greater intimacy with God; a greater appreciation of your design and gifts; enhanced, loving relationships with family and friends; complete freedom from fear and anxiety; and, a new assignment.

My Journal Notes

DAY STEWARDSHIP

"His lord said to him, 'Well done, good and faithful servant; you have been faithful over a few things, I will make you ruler over many things. Enter into the joy of your lord.'"

— MATTHEW 25:23 NKJV

It's interesting how the world views stewardship. Most treat the possessions of others with far less regard than the things they own. This is especially evident in the workplace. Behaving like the wicked steward who embezzled his master's money, many take work supplies for personal use or waste them without a thought. Time on the clock is spent chatting, playing on the Internet and daydreaming. The command *"Thou shalt not steal"* isn't even a consideration. Rented properties, equipment and vehicles are treated with neglect and disregard because they are someone else's problem.

The concept of ownership reveals another big difference between God's Kingdom and the world. Many focus on accumulating possessions and will use people to get things. You, on the other hand, are directed to use things to get people, to expend resources for Kingdom purposes. Getting caught up in the pursuit of possessions is an Enemy trap. Staying away from the owner mindset is a great protection against this.

Jesus makes it clear that you are to be a good steward over every resource you're given, because everything belongs to the Master and nothing is your own. Furthermore, according to the Parable of the Talents (Luke 17:19), it is the manner in which servants steward their master's resources that determine their reward. You work for the Lord. Everything you have belongs to Him and every action you take reflects on Him. In the workplace your employer is to be treated as if He were the Lord and you the faithful steward. There are no exceptions to these instructions. If you understand this...

Speak it out:

- All that I have and all that I am belongs to God. I surrender all my "rights" related to ownership.

- My body is a temple of the Holy Spirit and my mind is the entrance to my heart. I treat both with great care as their steward.

- By faith I trust that I too will receive more responsibility and authority as I am faithful over little.

Walk it out:

Stewarding Resources: Stewardship is a matter of making good use of *all* the resources you've been given. Time is perhaps the most precious. How are you spending your time these days? Are you still focusing effort on the daily things that will produce the legacy you hope to leave? If you have no income right now, are you tithing your time to the Body of Christ as is God's due? What about your stewardship over the temple of the Holy Spirit? Does your physical discipline and care demonstrate respect for the awesome gift of your body? Everything—your mind, talent, time, creativity and material possessions are all God's property entrusted to you. Will He find you faithful over all He has placed in your care when He returns?

My Journal Notes

DAY 5   PROMOTION

*"For all those who exalt themselves will be humbled,
and those who humble themselves will be exalted."*

- LUKE 18:13 NLT

Would you like a promotion at work? Why? If you're like the majority of workers, it's because you'd like more money, more influence, and perhaps a greater challenge. Truth be told, most aspire to promotion in hope of increased power, influence and pay. These, in turn, are expected to translate into a more comfortable life and increased happiness. Once again you see the worldly focus on self as the motivation behind career ambition.

Now look at Jesus' directions to His followers: *"Go into all the world and preach the gospel to every creature"* (Mark 16:15 NKJV) and *"Take care of my sheep"* (John 21:16). How might God view the purpose of a promotion that grants increased influence, income and responsibility? It's likely His purpose for increased influence is to bring greater numbers into right relationship with Jesus, isn't it? The purpose of a bigger income is to fuel increased generosity and a greater ability to bless others. *"And God is able to make all grace abound to you, so that in all things at all times, having all that you need, you will abound in every good work"* (2 Corinthians 9:8). As for a comfortable lifestyle—you won't find it in the Word. We're here to work as laborers in the harvest, and that's not easy work. Wherever you are assigned, God will provide your provision and supply all the resources required to get the job done.

God is the One who promotes, and He does so for His purposes. A Kingdom promotion could move you into a dark workplace in desperate need of His light. Finding yourself in such a circumstance is no indication that God doesn't care about you or your needs. He might actually be revealing His confidence in your ability to make a Kingdom difference in the darkness! Of course, a Kingdom promotion could also come with great financial reward. Don't be quick to rejoice in that. God is trusting you to guard your heart against the deceitfulness of riches, and that is a very tough assignment! In His wisdom God will decide when and how you are promoted. If you are willing to entrust your work future to Him…

SPEAK IT OUT:

· I trust God to lead me in the good works He prepared for me to accomplish.

· I know He makes all grace abound towards me, and I always have all sufficiency in all that I require.

· Promotion will come in God's perfect timing and in accordance with His will. My future is in His hands.

WALK IT OUT:

Keep Bouncing: Resilience is an important attribute in today's workplace. Jesus has promised to lead us in and out of good pastures. That means we're likely to experience change, doesn't it? Carefully read Mark, chapter 9, to hear how Jesus prepared disciples for their upcoming work. He sent them with absolutely nothing—no money, spare clothes or travel arrangements and yet, throughout their journey, they lacked for nothing. So expect to move and be placed in some uncomfortable assignments. You'll probably get knocked down, so determine to get back up. Prepare for change and stay flexible.

My Journal Notes

WEEK 11

KINGDOM PERFORMANCE

*"By myself I can do nothing; I judge only as I hear,
and my judgment is just, for I seek not to please myself
but him who sent me."*

- JOHN 5:30

You're entering the final weeks of your 90-day orientation, so it's performance appraisal time. According to Jesus in this verse, judgment that is just springs from the desire to please God. Therefore, you will be assessing yourself against what you have heard from the Father, through the words and example of His Son. First, you'll evaluate how the Kingdom is being displayed in your life, comparing yourself to a city set on a hill, shedding light in a dark world. Then you'll assess your Kingdom effectiveness in the workplace—as a "salt and light" influence that improves the quality of the work environment and enhances and preserves the lives of those you encounter.

Next, to check your vulnerability to the influences of the world, you'll review behaviors that render believers unfruitful and ineffective in accomplishing the objectives of the Kingdom. The big one, self-interest, will be the focus of attention since it ensnares so many believers in and out of the workplace. You'll be reminded to lift your eyes above the kingdoms of this world and maintain an eternal focus to avoid the self-centeredness trap. To protect you in the workplace, Paul offers this clear piece of advice: *"Therefore, since we are surrounded by such a great cloud of witnesses, let us throw off everything that hinders and the sin that so easily entangles. And let us run with perseverance the race marked out for us, fixing our eyes on Jesus, the pioneer and perfecter of faith..."* (Hebrews 12:1-2). Do you recognize this instruction? You've seen it before. It states again: Keep your eyes on Jesus and the storms of the workplace will not cause you to crumble. This week you'll assess how well you're doing in applying that guidance as you work.

Hopefully by now, you have grown in wisdom to know that any place outside of God's will and plan for you is somewhere you don't want to be. All the fruits of the Spirit are found in Christ and you cannot attain abundant life any other way. Finally, with spiritual maturity comes the capacity for self-judgment and correction. Exercise it and God won't need to chastise you as often as He did before Christ's character began to be formed in you. Just remember God's purpose is to have His children live the abundant life that He always intended. There is nothing He's inviting you into that isn't for the purpose of blessing you and giving you great joy.

C.S. Lewis sums up the journey towards God's Kingdom in this way: "The Scotch catechism says that man's chief end is 'to glorify God and enjoy Him forever.' But we shall then know that these are the same thing. Fully to enjoy is to glorify. In commanding us to glorify Him, God is inviting us to enjoy Him." [22] As you enter this week of self-evaluation...

 ## SPEAK IT OUT:

- By faith I increase in Christlikeness as I yield to the sanctifying work of the Holy Spirit in me.

- My loyalty in not divided. I resist the Enemy and all the temptations of this world and aim only for treasure that is eternal.

---

[22] C.S. Lewis, *Reflections on the Psalms*, Harcourt, Brace & World, New York, NY, 1958, pp. 96-97.

· I daily experience the love God has for me, and I pour that love out on others.

My Journal Notes

DAY 1   KINGDOM CRITERIA

"You are the salt of the earth. But what good is salt if it has lost its flavor? Can you make it salty again? It will be thrown out and trampled underfoot as worthless."

- MATTHEW 5:13 NLT

Salt is beneficial to human life—it flavors and preserves whenever added to foods. This scripture indicates that those who listen to and observe the teachings of Jesus will have this effect on the society around them. The same is true of Christ followers in the workplace. You are called to make a difference, for the good, in whatever organizations you may find yourself. Life should be better where you work simply because you're there. It is amazing how food that seems tasteless can become delicious with the addition of salt. Think what your impact can be on the lives of your co-workers if you constantly seek to bring out the best in them!

Notice that salt is a preservative too—it keeps food from spoiling and increases its usefulness and value. Can you say that you preserve those around you, that you keep them from being destroyed, physically and spiritually? Do you speak up for others when they are the butt of jokes or the target of ugly gossip? Has the witness of your life brought anyone closer to the Lord? The way that you respond to the storms of life can have that effect, you know. So reflecting on your behaviors, how do you measure up as salt in the workplace?

It's interesting that Jesus suggests that salt can lose its characteristic nature and become worthless. Apparently this happens when the salt no longer makes an enhancing and preserving difference. Perhaps this is the logical outcome when believers try so hard to "fit in" that they stop demonstrating the good news of the Gospel of Jesus Christ. Remember, your conversation is to be seasoned with salt and full of grace (Colossians 4:6). You are expected to forgive and keep on forgiving. You are even expected to serve every boss as if you are working for Jesus himself (Ephesians 6:5). You are in the workplace to help and serve others and, in so doing, demonstrate Christ's love and mercy. With your presence God is "salting" your workplace and increasing its value. So, how salty have you been? Spice it up and...

 ## SPEAK IT OUT:

- I am an ambassador for Jesus Christ and a representative for the Kingdom of God.

- Within me is the Kingdom of God, growing and transforming the workplace where I am planted.

- I worship God with my life and my witness.

 ## WALK IT OUT:

Take No Offense: If you're looking for a way to measure your progress in "dying to self," just pay attention to how often and how easily you get offended. Dead men don't get their feelings hurt! Believers are to avoid both giving offense and taking offense. So, whether you are justified or not, you are simply to stay out of the "offense business." Apologize if you've given any offense and forgive if you've taken any. Clear the offense record in your life, today.

My Journal Notes

DAY DERAILERS

"I am the resurrection and the life. He who believes in me will live, even though he dies; and whoever lives and believes in me will never die. Do you believe this?"

- JOHN 11:25-26

Here it is again… another message where Jesus tells you that you must die in order to live. Do you understand this instruction now? The flesh, "self" or ego that you've carried around with you in the workplace has got to go! There is no place in God's Kingdom for workers who have their focus on themselves. In the workplace the term "derailer" refers to behaviors that are so destructive and disruptive to the organization that they ruin careers and cost workers their jobs despite their great talent and skill. Arrogance, inflexibility and unwillingness to change are but a few. There are derailers in the Kingdom too, and as you might have guessed, they all have a basis in the "self" that needs to die. A few of the big ones are:

- Competition—the "me first" desire to win at someone else's expense

- Covetousness—the "that should have been mine" thinking that breeds resentment and dissatisfaction

- Criticism—the superior and self-righteous mindset that is comfortable rendering judgments about others

- Comparison—the "how am I doing compared to everyone else?" concern that fuels attention-seeking behaviors on one end of the continuum and withdrawal into poor self-esteem at the other

- Conformity—the desire to fit in and be approved of by others to the degree that integrity and Kingdom standards are compromised in the attempt

Every one of these mindsets is fueled by self-interest and self-focus. Notice too that they are all common behaviors, generally accepted and even promoted in the world. In fact, to behave otherwise will definitely single you out as different. And that's the goal of the Kingdom—to be different in a way that draws attention and brings glory to God. Get your eyes off yourself once and for all, trust God to watch out for your best interests and...

 SPEAK IT OUT:

· I align my will with the will of God. My focus is on His living Word.

· By faith and with the help of the Holy Spirit I put my flesh to death and live by the Spirit

· At Jesus' command I refuse to fear. I dwell in the shelter of the Most High and rest in the shadow of the Almighty. (Psalm 91)

WALK IT OUT:

Talking about Others: The workplace is filled with gossip, rumors and hurtful communications. Visit any lunchroom in the workplace, listen in on the conversation and chances are you'll hear people saying negative and unkind things. Are you guilty of this behavior? Colossians 4:6 gives this instruction to you: *"Let your conversation be always full of grace, seasoned with salt, so that you may know how to answer everyone."* As salt and light in the workplace, do your words show grace and mercy? Make sure you add only flavorful seasoning to the conversations in which you participate.

My Journal Notes

DAY 3 — ETERNITY

"Do not labor for the food which perishes, but for the food which endures to everlasting life, which the Son of Man will give you, because God the Father has set His seal on Him."

- JOHN 6:27 NKJV

Has an eternal perspective infiltrated your mind and thoughts enough to change the way you view your work and the things you are now trying to accomplish? The laws of love, life and purpose that you've learned to apply to your work here govern life in Heaven too. They are the laws of God's Kingdom. The objective of this life experience is to prepare you for a leadership position in eternity. The parable of the master who will return as king and decide on the assignments based on his servants' use of his resources directly applies to you right now (Luke 19).

This understanding should have the effect of creating patient endurance in you. That's nothing like the hopeless resignation, or silent suffering, demonstrated by so many believers. Employment conditions and apparent setbacks encountered in the workplace are temporary. Christ's promise to you is eternal. And don't miss what Jesus says in Revelation 3:10, when the final trial comes that will test all the inhabitants of earth. *"Since you have kept my command to endure patiently, I will also keep you from the hour of trial that is going to come upon the whole world to test those who live on the earth."* He will personally stand in for those who endure to the end. Your willingness to serve Him now with patient and faithful service will pay a big return on that day.

The apostle Paul states this about himself: *"I have learned the secret of being content in any and every situation, whether well fed or hungry, whether living in plenty or in want. I can do everything through him who gives me strength"* (Philippians 4:12-13). Obviously, focusing on Jesus and eternal life will keep and strengthen you in this life. The added bonus is that, with patient endurance and an eternal perspective, comes a contentment that can be found no other way. You are in the "home stretch"—on a journey to life with the Master in His eternal Kingdom. If you are beginning to comprehend this...

SPEAK IT OUT:

· I trust the timing of the Lord and wait on Him in peace and with patience.

· By faith I let patience have its perfect work in my life. I am complete in Christ and lacking nothing. (James 1:4)

· As I wait I will worship God with my life and confidently declare my faith in Him.

WALK IT OUT:

Accomplishment Statements: What have you accomplished in your work endeavors? How is the workplace better because you have been in it? Employers expect you to give descriptions of quantifiable contributions you have made to the company's objectives. God expects you to demonstrate His love to others and to lead them by example to His grace. Given the instruction, *"Feed my sheep"* (John 21:17), what have you accomplished? Whose life has been improved and who knows Christ better because of you? There's a great deal at stake.

My Journal Notes

DAY 4   **SELF-ASSESSMENT**

"I have brought you glory on earth by completing the work you gave me to do."

- JOHN 17:4

There is nothing easy about walking out a life that brings God glory, nothing easy about a battlefield assignment. By responding with immediate obedience to whatever direction He gives, you will glorify Him and finish your work. Obedience, after all, is the only thing that is truly yours to give. Every other thing, from your talents and skills to your opportunities to use them, was given to you by God. Using your free will to surrender to Him is the only way you can demonstrate your love for God.

As you open yourself to self-assessment expect the Holy Spirit to reveal disobedience and unbelief in your life. This is part of the sanctification process and it is always in your best interest. Use the conviction as your cue to confess, ask God for forgiveness, and repent. Jesus has already paid the price for your sins so allow honest self-assessment to increase your gratitude for the gift of redemption you have received. Remember, *"there is now no condemnation for those who are in Christ Jesus"* (Romans 8:1).

To accurately assess yourself, you must also understand that it isn't up to you to decide what brings God glory and pleases Him. He alone is the One who hands out the work assignments. God may place you in front of business leaders or hide you in a broom closet; He may showcase you in the workplace or ask you to be a powerful witness in a long season of unemployment. Let go of trying to determine when and how you'd like to serve Him and willingly follow in the footsteps of Jesus, finishing the work you're assigned no matter what it costs you.

Of course, chances are very good that your obedience will go completely unnoticed by others in the workplace. Those who do notice may think you are a fool to allow others to take advantage of you without making any attempts to defend or promote yourself. There is nothing about this life that will feel good to your natural self either. Doing unassigned, "godly" things to feel good about yourself is also disobedient, even though only you and God will know that your motive was personal satisfaction. He will get glory when you do what He has assigned you to do. If you are ready to work in the Body of Christ fulfilling your God-given purpose...

 SPEAK IT OUT:

· Thank you, God, for how you designed me and for establishing a perfect plan and work assignment for me.

· I walk in obedience to the will of God as my gift of love for Him.

· By faith I follow the leading of the Holy Spirit and live to finish the work my Father has given me to do.

 WALK IT OUT:

Behavior Audit: Take an audit of your current, or former, work behaviors in light of Kingdom standards. Judge yourself honestly. Use 2 Peter 1:5-8 as your guide. How do you measure up in moral excellence, knowledge, self-control, patient endurance, godliness, brotherly affection and love for everyone? Make a written list of your shortcomings, failures and character flaws, confess them before the Lord, and burn the paper up as a demonstration of your acceptance of God's forgiveness. Now ask the Holy Spirit to empower you to walk in obedience. Take every opportunity to practice, in and out of the workplace, so that you can bring God glory.

My Journal Notes

DAY GLORY

"He who speaks on his own does so to gain
honor for himself, but he who works for the honor
of the one who sent him is a man of truth;
there is nothing false about him."

- JOHN 7:18

Yesterday you saw how important obedience is in Kingdom employment. You also saw how easy it is to have mixed motives when serving God. You can always find "good things" to do but you may entirely miss what God has in mind for you if you go off without Him. In today's scripture Jesus focuses attention, one more time, on surrender and integrity.

In the workplace and in the Church today there are those who intentionally mislead others for personal gain. They manipulate the Word of God and use His name to try to bend people to their will. Still others mistakenly believe that they are so aligned with God that they don't even need to consult with Him about their decisions. Be wary of statements like "I know God would never want me to..." or "I don't need to ask God about this, I'm sure He..." That's how you fall into the trap of "religious thinking" and become self-deceived. You can guard against this by staying close enough to God to hear from Him directly and continuously.

It's also easy to slip into the ranks of the many believers who desire to glorify God their way. They want Him to be pleased with whatever they choose to give Him. This may explain why there are so many exhausted and miserable believers in the workplace—they're out of place and knocking themselves out "doing good" instead of "doing God." Although they may not realize it, they too have personal interests mixed into their motives.

The final word in your orientation performance appraisal is simply this, live your life in complete obedience to God's will and for His glory alone. No matter how noble your own plans might be, surrender them and allow God to direct your life. If you only desire to bring God glory by serving His will and purposes...

SPEAK IT OUT:

· I trust God to give me my assignments and bring Him glory through my obedience.

· I stand before the Lord in integrity. I have nothing to hide from my loving Father.

· My motives are pure. The Holy Spirit gives me discernment and keeps me on the path of righteousness.

WALK IT OUT:

Why Should I Hire You? Why do you deserve this promotion? If the question concludes any discussion of employment, use the opportunity to highlight the key criteria the employer is interested in—demonstrating that you listened carefully and are intent on meeting the employer's needs. Remember that character matters more than competence when you are building trust, so emphasize attributes like dependability and service over specific skill sets. Your response to this type of question provides another opportunity for you to examine the purity of your motives. Never (with God or man!) answer this question by stating how the position will satisfy your personal objectives. Focus completely on others and meeting their needs.

Remember, God has you covered; keep your focus on service and excellence to bring God glory in all you do.

My Journal Notes

KINGDOM COMPENSATION

"Behold, I am coming soon! My reward is with me, and I will give to everyone according to what he has done."

— REVELATION 22:12

Let's begin this week with a review of the "compensation" God would like to shower upon His children. This has been His intention since the days of Abraham and is still His desire for you today.

"The Lord will open the heavens, the storehouse of his bounty, to send rain on your land in season and to bless all the work of your hands. You will lend to many nations but will borrow from none. The Lord will make you the head, not the tail. If you pay attention to the commands of the Lord your God that I give you this day and carefully follow them, you will always be at the top, never at the bottom. Do not turn aside from any of the commands I give you today, to the right or to the left, following other gods and serving them" (Deuteronomy 28:12-14).

Pretty awesome, isn't it? Countless lives have proven that God richly rewards obedience and service in His Kingdom. Certainly there are those He has blessed financially in this life but there are also countless others who believed in His promises without seeing the realization of them in this world.

(Hebrews 11:13) That said, it is only Almighty God who has the ability to provide compensation that extends *beyond this world* and is *eternally valuable*. His guaranteed compensation package begins now and continues forever. In contrast, even the greatest pay package offered by a worldly employer will still be left behind in its entirety when you leave this earth. God's children must focus on the life beyond this for a right understanding of the "Kingdom pay plan."

Still, God has promised to provide for our every need while we're in this world, and so much more. In Jesus you'll receive forgiveness, confidence, wisdom, peace, joy—the list goes on and on. His eternal promises are worth any price you may be asked to pay in this life. God even has an eternal investment program. In serving the Kingdom you can actually build up a treasure account in Heaven (Matthew 6:20). "*...Fire will test the quality of each man's work. If what has been built survives, he will receive his reward. If it is burned up, he will suffer loss; he himself will be saved, but only as one escaping through the flames*" (1 Corinthians 3:13-15). Nothing in the world can even come close to God's abundant provisions for His employees.

This week you'll learn how you'll be paid as a Kingdom employee. You'll look at the recognition program God has in place as well as the rewards of prayer, giving and surrender. You'll discover that you play an active part in the determination of your compensation. And you'll realize that the key to success is to forget about "what's in it for me" and live a life of intimacy with the Lord and service to others. Trust God, the rewards will be greater than you can imagine, in this life and the next.

As soon as you are ready to take your eyes off temporary things that decay and fade away...

 ## SPEAK IT OUT:

· By faith I will bring God glory in this life and present my Lord with crowns in the next.

· I know that God is the perfect Father. I trust myself in His care.

· I follow after Jesus not for personal gain but out of my love for all He does for me.

My Journal Notes

DAY RECOGNITION

"Watch out! Don't do your good deeds publicly,
to be admired by others, for you will lose the
reward from your Father in heaven."

- MATTHEW 6:1 NLT

You'd be hard pressed to find a scripture that differs more from the practices of the workplace than this one. Wherever you work you're likely to find people trying to make sure they get credit not only for their "good work" but even for the work of others. Many won't do good deeds at all if no one is watching, dismissing the opportunity with the comment "What's the point?"

A quick search through the gospels makes it very clear that God's recognition program is only for those who have lost all interest in gaining the approval and recognition of men. God is all about *secret and private rewards,* as you'll see over the next few days. You'll have to choose between the public rewards and recognition of the world or His Kingdom recognition—you can't have it both ways. On the other hand, Max Lucado offers this insight into the Father's recognition system: "Some of you have never won a prize in your life...All you have are 'almosts' and 'what ifs.' If that hits home then you'll cherish this promise. *'And when the Chief Shepherd appears, you will receive the crown of glory that will never fade away'* (1 Peter 5:4). Your day is coming. What the world has overlooked, your Father has remembered and, sooner than you can imagine, you will be blessed by Him."[23]

Get started in the Kingdom recognition process by giving the Lord all the credit He's due. *"I tell you, whoever publicly acknowledges me before others, the Son of Man will also acknowledge before the angels of God"* (Luke 12:8). If

---

[23] Max Lucado, The Lucado Inspirational Reader, Thomas Nelson, Nashville, TN, 2011, p. 304.

you've made comments like "You'll have to forgive me. God isn't finished with me yet," realize that you've credited God with your inadequacies and failures. Are you equally quick or quicker to credit Him for all your accomplishments and contributions? Whenever an opportunity presents itself, make sure you declare that *"Every good and perfect gift is from above"* (James 1:17) and...

SPEAK IT OUT:

- I publicly acknowledge that all creative ideas and abilities to perform my work with excellence come from God.

- I am designed by God for good works, and I give Him all the glory for what I accomplish.

- I am empowered by the Holy Spirit every day in all I do, and I am grateful.

WALK IT OUT:

Defense against Offense: *"And blessed is he who is not offended because of me"* (Matthew 11:6). As you've worked through this orientation program you may have encountered instructions that you really didn't like or want to obey. Jesus' commands to forgive and to serve are hard to take. You may also find that the "rewards" you were hoping for, in exchange for your obedience, are just not coming fast enough. Don't fall into the trap of judging God or getting offended at Jesus. God's Word is true and His rewards are guaranteed. They may not look like what you're expecting or happen in the timing you wish, but remember, God has His eye on your entire, eternal life. His focus is on making you perfect and complete, not comfortable. He sees what you cannot see and is preparing you for a life you don't yet know. Trust Him.

My Journal Notes

REWARDS OF PRAYER

"But you, when you pray, go into your room, and when you have shut your door, pray to your Father who is in the secret place; and your Father who sees in secret will reward you openly."

— MATTHEW 6:6 NKJV

"At daybreak, Jesus went out to a solitary place."

— LUKE 4:42

"Once when Jesus was praying in private and his disciples were with him..."

— LUKE 9:18

Many ignore the behavior Jesus modeled and simply disregard His command to seek God in a "secret place." They don't spend time alone with their Lord on a consistent basis and their lives suffer as a result. Imagine your employer offering you a one-on-one meeting every morning to review the day's priorities and concerns and you announce you're not interested in attending. How long would you expect to be successful in that position?

Prayer is your opportunity to fellowship with God; to bask in His presence and hear from the Source about specific situations in your life. If you're seeking the Kingdom, how can you turn down a daily audience with the King? Peter makes an important comment: *"He who comes to God must believe that He is, and that He is a rewarder of those who diligently seek Him"* (Hebrews 11:6 NKJV). Many believers understand that God is real but miss out on the rewards of diligent seeking.

Believe God will provide something of great value whenever you come to Him. When you stop seeking the *presents of God* and go after the *presence of God* your life will be radically transformed. The peace and joy experienced in His presence is priceless. Abide in Him and find yourself being transformed into His image. It's true that you become like those with whom you closely associate. Beyond these wonderful rewards, expect God to tell you what to ask Him for and what actions to take each day so that He might lead you into the good works and future He has prepared for you. "Prayer is not simply getting things from God—that is only the most elementary kind of prayer. Prayer is coming into perfect fellowship and oneness with God. If the Son of God has been formed in us through regeneration then He will continue to press on beyond our common sense and will change our attitude about the things for which we pray."[24] If you desire the rewards of secret prayer and the opportunity to be changed by God in prayer...

SPEAK IT OUT:

- I seek the will of God. I want my words and desires to match those of my King.

- By faith I accept God at His word and seek His desires for my life.

- I willingly release all of my demands and invite God to fill me as He chooses.

---

[24] Oswald Chambers, *My Utmost for His Highest*, Discovery House Publishers, Grand Rapids, MI, 1992, Devotional for September 16.

WALK IT OUT:

Remembrance Journal: Ever notice how easy it is to remember hurts and offenses and how hard it is to recall all the great things you've experienced? John the Baptist heard the audible voice of God saying that Jesus was His Son. And yet, in prison, John experienced a crisis of doubt. When John's disciples came to question Jesus, He simply sent them back to remind John of the miraculous things they had seen Him do. Great advice. Get a journal and train yourself to write down every "God sighting" you can recall …the bill that was half the size you expected, the tank of gas that lasted three weeks, the reduction in your house payment, the unexpected refund. Then, when you're tempted to think God has forgotten you, look at what you've written.

My Journal Notes

My Journal Notes

DAY 3   REWARDS OF GIVING

"But when you give to the needy, do not let
your left hand know what your right hand is doing,
so that your giving may be in secret. Then your Father,
who sees what is done in secret, will reward you."

- MATTHEW 6:3-4

Giving is essential in God's compensation program and the rewards for giving start with you— giving in gratitude for what God has already done! Notice that Jesus says "when" you give, not "if." Here He explains more about God's reward for giving that's initiated by gratitude and obedience: *"Give, and it will be given to you. A good measure, pressed down, shaken together and running over, will be poured into your lap. For with the measure you use, it will be measured to you"* (Luke 6:38). This is not a promise that if you give $100 to the poor, you will receive $100. It simply means that if you give with a full measure, God will pour a full measure of His blessing on you. John Wesley put it this way, "Do all the good you can, By all the means you can, In all the ways you can, In all the places you can, At all the times you can, To all the people you can, As long as ever you can." [25] Keep your focus on pouring out, not gathering in.

By the way, tithing is not giving. All you can do with the first 10 percent of your income is return it to God or steal it, for it belongs to the Lord (Leviticus 27:30). If you aren't covering your bills with 100% of your income, try it God's way and see what He'll do with your 90 percent! Study the promise of Malachi 3:10—the open windows of Heaven and God's rebuke of the devourer—and "put God to the test."

---

[25] John Wesley, *Letters of John Wesley*, ed. George Eayrs, Kessinger Publishing, Whitefish, MT, 2007, p. 423.

But don't bother to give or tithe out of legalism or constraint. Cheerful giving in response to God's love is the condition of the heart required to receive rewards from the heavenly Father as Jesus promised (2 Corinthians 9:6-8). If you'd like to spend your life trying to out-give God...

Speak it out:

· I live to give and know that my Father does the same!

· By faith I believe all my needs are met by God, so I can focus on giving to others.

· I work hard in order to bless others and show God's love to them.

Walk it out:

Pass It On... What do you have to give? Clothes you're not wearing, household items you're not using? Give them away and bless someone. If you have nothing to give, extend a helping hand. Perhaps a neighbor needs help with physical chores or a single mom could use a hand cleaning her house. Find a need and take care of it today. Next, find out who in your church family is in the job market right now. Make sure you keep their work objectives in mind everywhere you go. Set a goal to find at least one lead for each job seeker every week. Sharing leads is one of the very best investments you can make in your own current, or future, job search process. *"Give and it will be given to you...."*

My Journal Notes

DAY 4 REWARDS OF SURRENDER

"'I tell you the truth,' Jesus replied, 'no one who has left home or brothers or sisters or mother or father or children or fields for me and the gospel will fail to receive a hundred times as much in this present age (homes, brothers, sisters, mothers, children and fields—and with them persecutions) and in the age to come, eternal life.'"

- Mark 10:29-30

The disciples left everything behind, and they wanted to know what they would receive for surrendering all. Today's scripture is Jesus' answer. Plain and simple, He declared they would receive a hundredfold return. (And He promised ongoing persecutions for the duration of the present age.) But this isn't a promise of worldly riches for personal gain—it's a promise of support and resources to sustain the mission of a surrendered life. You'll notice that none of the disciples cashed in and spent the rest of their lives on the golf course.

When you catch fire for the sake of the Gospel, Jesus will see to it that you have everything you need to keep that fire burning. He sent the disciples out with no money, clothes or accommodations, to preach the Good News. They came back weeks later rejoicing in the experience. Jesus asked *"When I sent you without purse, bag or sandals, did you lack anything?' 'Nothing,' they answered"* (Luke 22:35). Their needs had been covered but their focus wasn't on material things, they were busy being thrilled at the results of their Kingdom service!

"For the Son of Man is going to come in his Father's glory with his angels, and then he will reward each person according to what he has done" (Matthew

16:27). When all you want is to keep going for the glory of God, expect a hundredfold spiritual expense account to get the job done and...

SPEAK IT OUT:

- I give my all to Jesus because He gave His all for me.

- My eyes are fixed on the destiny God has for me. Worldly riches and material gain cannot distract me.

- I trust the Lord to meet all my needs. I am rich in my life in Him.

WALK IT OUT:

Obstacle Course: Today you can assess your level of trust in God and His ability to overcome the obstacles that stand between you and your next work assignment. What, from your past, might be holding you back—lack of education, unprofessional image, bad habits, or missing job search skills? Whatever it may be, now is the time to implement a strategy to overcome it. First, change your mind. Stop viewing it as insurmountable. Trust that God has already made a way over, around or through it! Next get help from a trusted advisor and create a plan to deal with the issues and obstacles you face. There is always a way out for an obedient child of God. Just realize this, God is full of surprises and sometimes the way out is a path in an entirely different direction!

My Journal Notes

ABUNDANT LIFE

"I have come that they may have life, and that they may have it more abundantly."

- JOHN 10:10 NKJV

When you began this Orientation process what did the term "abundant life" mean to you? Were you thinking like a citizen of the world and wondering when your wealth was going to appear? How about now? Have you come to realize that you are already walking in the Kingdom of God and are rich beyond measure?

The abundant life promised by Jesus, started for you before your birth, will spill out into an eternity in His loving presence. In your mother's womb God knew you and designed you for a Kingdom purpose and destiny. He counted the cost of your life on earth and established a heavenly supply covering all you'll ever need in to accomplish your purpose. Then, out of His love and delight in you, He planned some wonderful surprises as well... glorious sunsets, loving relationships, dreams and opportunities, and so much more. This earthly life cannot contain the fullness of abundant life.

The world is filled with people who have an abundance of money and material things but are experiencing poor health and broken relationships. They are just poor people with money. There are also people whose needs are met, yet they suffer with envy and continuous fear of lack. All of them are consumed with the desire to "improve their lot in life," because they have no vision of anything beyond this world. Their greatest poverty is that they exist with no loving, heavenly Father to sustain them now and see nothing but death in their future. What price would these citizens of the world place on perfect peace, freedom from fear and worry, true acceptance and an eternity in heaven? Yet these are just the by-products of a life centered in the love of Jesus Christ. Far more wonderful is knowing Jesus personally and being known and loved by Him—now and forever. If you are beginning to grasp this amazing truth...

SPEAK IT OUT:

- I thank God for the gift of abundant life. Every day I experience His great love for me.

- I have eternal life and the Kingdom of God growing within me now. My future is secure.

- By the power of the Holy Spirit I share the Gospel of Jesus Christ with others, that they might know Him and experience salvation.

WALK IT OUT:

To Do List: By now I hope you recognize that your abundant life is already happening. As you focus on the perfect, awesome love of Jesus for you, your heart should be overflowing with a desire to do something to show your love for Him. Stay in His presence until you experience this desire. Ask Him to become more real to you every day so that His love will fill your heart to overflowing. Then make your "To Do" list for Jesus. Scan your workplace looking for His sheep that need feeding. Find the lost and bring them to Him. Don't let a day pass when you don't share your wealth!

My Journal Notes

KINGDOM JUMP START

> *"This, then, is how you should pray: 'Our Father in heaven, hallowed be your name, your kingdom come, your will be done, on earth as it is in heaven. Give us today our daily bread. Forgive us our debts, as we also have forgiven our debtors. And lead us not into temptation, but deliver us from the evil one.'"*

> - MATTHEW 6:9-13

Jesus recognized that His disciples needed some help with their prayer life, so He provided them with a model that you will recognize as The Lord's Prayer. By His death and resurrection, Jesus completely fulfilled every one of its requests. He provides our daily bread, offers us forgiveness, and delivers us from sin and death. "This prayer reminds us that we are to ask for the meeting of our particular personal needs as a means to our Father's glory, and not in any spirit of trying to bend God's will to our own." [26]

At the start of each day, the Lord's Prayer can be your reminder of all that Jesus has already done for you. It's one thing to feel connected to God in church or alone in a time of prayer. It's another matter entirely to

---

[26] J.I. Packer, *Growing in Christ*, Crossway/Good News Publishers, Wheaton, IL, 1994, p. 23.

maintain that awareness and sense of connection amidst the pressures of the workplace or the complete uncertainty of a job search process. So as you come to the end of your Kingdom orientation process, this week you'll focus on the Lord's Prayer and all that it reinforces about your true Kingdom status.

Make it your habit to spend time every morning reflecting on Truth and your eternal inheritance by following the pattern of this perfect prayer. Line by line and concept by concept it offers a Kingdom reminder that will jump-start your workday and keep you in perfect peace. Let this overview remind you of:

His Sovereignty: Your Father in Heaven stands outside of time and worldly circumstances. Every situation you encounter, every person you interact with, and everything you experience is already known to Him and He has you covered.

His Name: The great I AM is holy and worthy of reverence. His character is revealed in His name and in all the wonderful ways He has demonstrated His love for His children. Now, through the gift of His Son, you have been granted the privilege of using the name above every name, Jesus.

His Will: His plan for His Kingdom to come into the earth is now being realized and you play a significant part in God's purposes.

His Provision: Your daily bread has already been provided. God will always supply all your needs according to the riches of His glory in Christ Jesus.

His Protection: The Enemy has been conquered through the finished work of Jesus (2 Corinthians 2:14). Christ has overcome the world and in Him you have victory and freedom.

SPEAK IT OUT:

- As a citizen of the Kingdom of God I work to do His will on earth.

- I live by the laws of His Kingdom and trust in God's provision and protection.

- I thank you, Lord, that all I need has already been provided. I receive it with gratitude and do not covet more than You are willing to provide.

My Journal Notes

My Journal Notes

DAY 1 HIS SOVEREIGNTY

*"And now, Father, glorify me in your presence
with the glory I had with you before the world began."*

- JOHN 17:5

"Our Father in heaven…" How important is it that you have a Father who stands outside of time in a spiritual Kingdom called heaven? In the gospel of Matthew, Jesus refers to God as His "Father in heaven" a dozen times. Clearly He felt this was important for you to know. Each day, before you start work, think about what this truth means.

Heaven is God's vantage point. Nothing about your life or circumstances will ever surprise God. Nothing will ever happen to you that God has not already seen and dealt with for your best interest. The psalmist clearly understood the value of this gift when he stated: *"In God I trust; I will not be afraid. What can man do to me?"* (Psalm 56:11) Jesus will always lead you in triumph. He cares for every detail of your life because He loves you perfectly. When nothing makes sense and you don't know where to turn, God's got your back. You have Friends in high places!

Heaven is your Source. No matter what happens in the systems of the world or its economy, you are secure. Everything you need will be provided from God's endless supply. The same God who provided manna and springs in the desert is watching over you. The One who spoke all of creation into being from His heavenly realm has you covered.

Heaven is your home and final destination. In Christ, you have inherited the Kingdom of God and your future is assured. *"Let not your heart be troubled; you believe in God, believe also in Me. In My Father's house are many mansions; if it were not so, I would have told you. I go to prepare a place for you. And if I go and prepare a place for you, I will come again and receive you to Myself; that where I am, there you may be also"* (John 14:1-3 NKJV). In light of eternity, your time on Earth will be short. Keep your eyes on Jesus and your final destination whenever the journey gets tough. If you trust when all is said and done that your Father in heaven will have the final word...

Speak it out:

· My future is assured, and I am safe in God's hands.

· I trust God for the promise of heaven, and I trust Him to care for me now.

· I am Christ's ambassador, and my needs are supplied by His Kingdom.

Walk it out:

Comfort for Coworkers: *"Comfort, comfort my people, says your God"* (Isaiah 40). Are you doing that in the workplace? This isn't referring to sympathizing or commiserating, but the offering of true comfort. The world can't offer comfort because it requires a faith in God and confidence in heaven to make the promises comfort requires. When a crisis or personal tragedy hits, be the first one to offer prayer, peace and support. Jesus will show up when you do.

My Journal Notes

DAY 2   HIS NAME

> *"For where two or three come together in my name,*
> *there am I with them."*
>
> - MATTHEW 18:20

"Hallowed be your name" (Matthew 6:9). Spend time meditating on the name of God. Let it really soak into your heart and mind that He is the great I AM. He existed before the beginning of time and remains unchanged today. He will still exist when time ceases. He is the One who holds you and your future in His hands.

Reflect on all the names men have assigned to Him—Almighty, Healer, Provider, Victory Banner, King of Kings.... Each name tells of His character and His great love for you. Allow His name to bring you into worship, for He alone is worthy. Remember as you go through your day that the God you serve is all knowing, all powerful, all wise and all loving. There is no place outside of His presence and nothing you do will change His perfect love for you. He is love and light and life.

Now turn your attention to the name of Jesus. *"Therefore God exalted him to the highest place and gave him the name that is above every name, that at the name of Jesus every knee should bow, in heaven and on earth and under the earth, and every tongue confess that Jesus Christ is Lord, to the glory of God the Father"* (Philippians 2:9-11). You have been given this awesome name to use as the Father directs. But let's be clear about what this means. "In the name of Jesus" is not some incantation that you can slap on any request and cause it to materialize. To ask in the name of Jesus means that you are making a request that Jesus Himself would be willing to carry to the Father on your behalf. The Lord was very clear about His criteria for effectual prayer. The request should glorify the Father (John 14:13), the fulfilled request should produce lasting fruit for the Kingdom (John 15:16), and the one praying should not "ask amiss" for the sake of selfish pleasures (James 4:3).

Remember—one key purpose of prayer is to hear from God and to find out what He would have you do. Once you get your marching orders you can move forward to accomplish them knowing that God Himself will back you up. With His Word you can believe and not doubt. Without it, you can do nothing! Walk in the power of His love and deep appreciation of His Name and...

 ## Speak it out:

- I know that I am a spirit being, created in the image of God and His precious Son.

- I worship God in spirit and in truth. My life is found in Him.

- By faith I trust in the name of Jesus for all I need. He is more than enough.

 ## Walk it out:

Proper Use of God's Name: In the workplace and world the name of Jesus and the phrase "Oh my God!" are common and casual exclamations. Where do you stand in all of this? Do you use the Lord's name as a blessing or to curse? Do you use the name of Jesus with intention and power? Do you call on God when you really mean it? Imagine the satisfaction the Enemy feels when he hears someone using God's name in vain. Don't give him pleasure (or satisfaction) through your careless use of God's holy name.

My Journal Notes

DAY 3   HIS WILL

"This is the will of the Father who sent Me,
that of all He has given Me I should lose nothing,
but should raise it up at the last day.
And this is the will of Him who sent Me, that
everyone who sees the Son and believes in Him
may have everlasting life."

- JOHN 6:39-40 NKJV

"Your kingdom come. Your will be done on earth as it is in heaven" (Matthew 6:10). You know this but it bears repeating—God loves you just as He does Jesus! You are His beloved child and it is His will to perfect you, making you complete and wanting nothing. He seeks a deep personal relationship with you. Trust Him and place your life in His hands. As you yield your life to the sanctifying power of the Holy Spirit, He will make you in the image and likeness of Christ. Never forget that God's will for you is good and only good. There is no safer place in which to abide than in His will.

It's also God's will that you participate in His eternal plan! You have been created to bring God glory through your service in His Body and the world. Some believers really struggle with this, fearing they'll make a choice or take and action displeasing to God. Allow this statement by A.W. Tozer to put your mind to rest. "The man or woman who is wholly or joyously surrendered to Christ can't make a wrong choice—any choice will be the right one."[27]

Never lose sight of what really matters. Some day you will see Jesus face

---

[27] A.W. Tozer, *Knowledge of the Holy: The Attributes of God: Their Meaning in the Christian Life*, Harper Collins, New York, NY, 1961, p. 70.

to face. If you've faithfully done His will, you'll hear the words, *"Well done, good and faithful servant! You have been faithful with a few things; I will put you in charge of many things. Come and share your master's happiness!"* (Matthew 25:23). What a celebration that will be! Rejoice now and...

SPEAK IT OUT:

· God's will for me is perfect and I surrender all that I am in service to it.

· I trust the Holy Spirit to lead me in the fulfillment of my God-given destiny.

· I thank God for the joy and privilege of citizenship in His Kingdom.

WALK IT OUT:

Take Any Job? There are two common ways that you can miss out on God's plan for your life. The first occurs when you look for new employment with the intention of just taking any job you can find whether it fits you or not. The second is to stay too long in a job that no longer serves your destiny resisting the urging of the Holy Spirit to leave your current assignment. Job seekers may take these actions because the job market doesn't appear promising enough to risk following the leading of the Holy Spirit. Those are not the trusting behaviors of a believer and representative of the Kingdom of God. How will it bring God glory for you to take, or stay in, a position He has planned for someone else? How can it be right to ask an employer to invest training and responsibility in you, or to continue to pay for your services when you have no intention of committing yourself in return? There are plenty of alternatives—take temporary work, be a contractor, or offer yourself where there is a need, but always be honest about your intentions when you accept work. Don't spend your time in a place that isn't meant for you.

My Journal Notes

DAY 4   HIS PROVISION

"Why are you talking about having no bread?
Do you still not see or understand?
Are your hearts hardened? Do you have eyes
but fail to see, and ears but fail to hear?"

- MARK 8:17-18

"Give us today our daily bread. Forgive us our debts" (Matthew 6:11-12). In the days of the Roman Empire, local rulers would give people bread to gain their loyalty. An ancient writer satirically referred to this practice as providing people with "bread and circuses."[28] Perhaps in response, Jesus directed His disciples to make their requests for bread, favor, and forgiveness only to God. Clearly He wanted the disciples to understand that God alone was their source of physical and spiritual provision. This is still His word to believers today.

And realize that God completely satisfied this prayer with Jesus—the Bread of Life—who forgives every sin and provides for every need. In today's scripture you can sense His frustration with His disciples because they hadn't figured out that, through Him, God would always supply their needs. *"I am the bread of life. He who comes to me will never go hungry, and he who believes in me will never be thirsty"* (John 6:35). He isn't saying that believers will never experience hunger or thirst—this happens every day to persecuted Christian brothers and sisters around the world. He's saying that some things are more important than food or water. He comes from a perspective that has visibility into the eternal realm that awaits us. He truly is the complete Provider and,

---

[28] "Panem et circenses" A phrase, by Juvenal (Satires, 10.77–81) referring to the Roman practice of providing free wheat and entertainment to Roman citizens as a means of gaining and sustaining political power.

in trusting Him, your needs will be met now and forever.

You do not need to be held hostage by the workplace any longer. You don't need to live in fear of a layoff or compromise your values to hang on to a bad job. You work for the same God that provided manna for His children in the wilderness and fed the multitudes with a little boy's lunch. He is still in the supernatural provision business. His promise in Matthew 6:31-33 still stands: *"So do not worry, saying, 'What shall we eat?' or 'What shall we drink?' or 'What shall we wear?' For the pagans run after all these things, and your heavenly Father knows that you need them. But seek first his kingdom and his righteousness, and all these things will be given to you as well."* No matter if your need is for rent, food, gasoline, healing, forgiveness or deliverance, He will always provide for your needs, so...

 ## SPEAK IT OUT:

· My God will supply all my needs according to His riches in Christ Jesus.

· By faith I accept Jesus as my Bread of life and my all sufficiency.

· The Lord God is my provider. I will not fear for what can man do to me?

 ## WALK IT OUT:

Expand Your Reach: Like it or not, you probably won't find a new work assignment or a more challenging position by sitting around waiting for the phone to ring or an email to pop up. Get out today and expand your network. Trust that God is working behind the scenes to prepare opportunities for you. Keep moving and you'll see God opening doors and making His provision available. While you're out in the marketplace, pray over business leaders, job seekers and places you visit. Intercede for the workplace. And, if you run out of ideas, contacts or energy, find a way to share your talents somewhere new, for free. Volunteer your time and gifts. Use your skills and talents to make a difference for the Kingdom.

My Journal Notes

DAY 5   HIS PROTECTION

"Holy Father, protect them by the power of your name—
the name you gave me—so that they may be one as we
are one.... My prayer is not that you take them out of the
world but that you protect them from the evil one."

- JOHN 17:11, 15

"And lead us not into temptation, but deliver us from the evil one" (Matthew 6:13). Jesus stripped the evil one of power and authority, but He didn't remove him from the world, or the workplace. Your Enemy is still very much at work deceiving, counterfeiting and misleading. Despite all the health and safety standards of men, the workplace is not safe. You may be exposed to acts of violence and physical danger as well as snares that can entrap you and pull you out from under God's protective covering. Jesus, your Supervisor, wants you to know this: *"I am sending you out like sheep among wolves. Therefore be as shrewd as snakes and as innocent as doves"* (Matthew 10:16). You must learn to be in the world and to understand the world; you just cannot become a part of the world.

Don't confuse the promise of God's eternal protection with being kept comfortable in this life, however. As you've already, seen believers are not exempt from the daily trials and hardships of this world. In fact these actually work to your benefit as you await your eternal inheritance, *"In this you greatly rejoice, though now for a little while you may have had to suffer grief in all kinds of trials. These have come so that your faith—of greater worth than gold, which perishes even though refined by fire—may be proved genuine and may result in praise, glory and honor when Jesus Christ is revealed"* (1 Peter 1:6-7).

While you're on Earth *"fight the good fight of faith"* (1 Timothy 6:12). Don't count on anything less and you won't be taken off guard. Just remember you have the greater One inside you (1 John 4:4) and the Enemy will flee whenever you resist him (James 4:7). You also have this promise to encourage you in the battle: *"All who are victorious will be clothed in white. I will never erase their names from the Book of Life, but I will announce before my Father and his angels that they are mine"* (Revelation 3:5 NLT). If you know you're safe in the Father's arms…

SPEAK IT OUT:

- By faith I claim my protection in Christ and accept the help of ministering angels God assigns me. (Psalm 91)

- I resist the devil and he must flee. I am covered by the blood of Jesus, the Enemy cannot harm me.

- I have no fear, worry or doubt. I cast my cares on God who cares for me.

WALK IT OUT:

Take Any Job? Do you know your own weaknesses, where you are vulnerable and can be tempted, especially at work? Some things should be obvious—there is no such thing as innocent flirting; it's never okay to lie about a mistake; and, knowingly participating in financial deception is always wrong. Your problem areas may be different. But whatever you struggle with, make sure you keep yourself as far from it as possible. To protect yourself, confess your weakness to another strong believer, ask for support and put yourself into an accountability relationship. The Holy Spirit will empower you to resist temptation, but you must also exercise choice and wisdom. Help yourself through distance and personal transparency. Don't forget, your effectiveness and greatest impact will likely be birthed from your experiences of brokenness and struggle.

My Journal Notes

EPILOGUE

Your Kingdom employment orientation is complete. Now the real adventure begins! It is my fervent prayer that you experienced a deepening and intimately personal relationship with God as you worked your way through this process. For my part, I remain constantly awed at the outrageous privilege we've been granted as followers of Jesus Christ. By His blood we've been invited into intimate fellowship with the One True God in three persons: the Heavenly Father—our true Employer; Jesus—our Lord, Master, Supervisor and Mentor; and the amazing, ever-present Holy Spirit—our Guide, Trainer and Advocate. Nothing will ever be more valuable than that relationship, in this life or the next!

As I see it, working every day, on the job or in an employment search, is a bit like hiking through an unfamiliar wood. At ground level you see the trees, landmarks, and underbrush surrounding you as you work your way forward. You can't really gauge your progress or your proximity to the goal from this perspective. But with today's technology you have the ability to find that same unfamiliar terrain in an aerial photograph and view it from a much different vantage point. The resulting change in perspective is amazing. Now you can see right where you were walking and what the bigger picture looks like. Working with a Kingdom employment perspective produces a similar dramatic change. Given the bigger, eternal vantage point, daily work comes into proper perspective when viewed in the context of divine destiny with a focus on the One who holds eternity in His hands! Perspective doesn't change the actual happenstances of life. You'll still encounter the trees that obscure your vision and some huge obstacles. Along the way there will still be stunning rainbows and annoying mosquitos; inclement weather and glorious sunshiny days. But if you have come up higher to a life in Christ Jesus the view from the Father's arms will continue to change your daily work and life until the glorious day when Jesus returns.

It was my sole intention to point you, every day, to the One who continues to make an extraordinary difference in the lives of job seekers, business owners and workers whenever they simply trust Him and obey. I've seen this more times than I can count in my own life and the lives of those I've prayed, studied and rejoiced with across the years.

There simply is no reason for believers to behave in the workplace as the world does, striving after the ways and means to care for themselves. Providing is God's part. Our part is to rest in the finished work of Jesus Christ and allow God to lead us in the way of His perfect will. The wonderful truth of life in Christ has been beautifully summed up by J.I. Packer in these few statements:

**"What were we made for? To know God.
What aim should we have in life? To know God.
What is the eternal life that Jesus gives? To know God.
What is the best thing in life? To know God."** [29]

It is my hope that this devotional has ignited and fueled a desire in you to "seek first" after the Kingdom, and the King, for the rest of your life. May your hunger and thirst for God position you to realize your Kingdom purpose and receive all that the loving Father has for you. And may you live a life of true worship in fellowship with the Lord now and forever!

---

[29] J.I. Packer, *Knowing God*, InterVarsity Press, Downers Grove, IL, 1973, p. 33.